Religion in focus
Christianity
in today's world

Claire Clinton

Sally Lynch

Janet Orchard

Deborah Weston

Angela Wright

Faith community editor

Sally Lynch

John Murray

Other titles in this series:
Islam in today's world ISBN 0 7195 7194 4
Judaism in today's world ISBN 0 7195 7197 9

Members of different Christian faith communities have been widely interviewed and consulted in the preparation of this book, although the authors take responsibility for the views expressed herein.

The authors particularly acknowledge the helpful advice of the following faith community consultants and educational consultants who have read and commented on this book at various stages of its development:
Lat Blaylock, Executive Officer for the Professional Council for Religious Education; **Janet Dyson**, Religious Education Adviser, Essex; **Revd Andrew J Faley**, National Adviser for Catechesis and Religious Education, Catholic Bishops' Conference of England and Wales; **Revd Professor Leslie J Francis**, Professor of Pastoral Theology, Trinity College, Carmarthen; **Phil Metcalf**, Religious Education Adviser, Somerset; **Roger Owen**, Chief Examiner, NEAB Syllabus D; **Elizabeth Templeton**, Development Officer for the Christian Education Movement, Scotland.

© Claire Clinton, Sally Lynch, Janet Orchard, Deborah Weston, Angela Wright 1998

First published 1998
by John Murray (Publishers) Ltd
50 Albemarle Street
London W1X 4BD

Reprinted 1998, 1999 (twice)

Artwork by Oxford Illustrators Ltd
Layouts by Amanda Hawkes
Typeset in Rockwell Light by Wearset, Boldon, Tyne and Wear
Printed and bound in the United Kingdom by the University Press, Cambridge

A CIP catalogue record for this book is available from the British Library.

ISBN 0 7195 7193 6

Contents

A
Introduction

B
Thinking
about morality

C
Thinking
about God

Acknowledgements

The authors would like to thank their families, friends and work colleagues for all their help, support and tolerance throughout the writing of this book.

The authors and publishers would also like to thank the following for their co-operation:

pp.28–9 Sue, Nasreen and Mary; pp.40–41 the Wells family; p.53 Right Revd John Sentamu; p.54 Revd Mother Ann Easter & Revd Father Christopher Owens; p.68 Sir John Templeton; p.79 Ken Edgar; p.97 Astrid; pp.98–9 John Rajah; p.110 Jonathan Edwards; pp.114, 118 pupils at St Bede's Comprehensive Church School, Cambridge; p.125 Dilly Baker.

The authors and publishers are grateful to the following for permission to include material in the text:

p.21 'The careful death of José' from the *New Internationalist*, April 1997; p.31 *Sources F & G* from *Slow Coming Dark* by Doug Magee © 1980 The Pilgrim Press, New York; p.32 *Source A* from *The Song of Songs that is Solomon's* published by The Ark Press; p.39 Extract from The Marriage Service in *The Alternative Service Book 1980* is copyright © The Central Board of Finance of the Church of England 1980 and is reproduced by permission; p.45 *Source A* from the *Church Times*; p.46 *Source B* from *What does the Bible say about homosexual practice?* © Tony Higton 1997, published by ABWON Ltd; p.49 *Source A* adapted from David Haslam, *Race for the Millenium* (Church House Publishing, 1996), published on behalf of the Churches' Commission for Racial Justice. Reproduced by permission; p.51 'Messiah Man' by Ben Okafor from *Racism: whose problem, whose decision?* published by the Scripture Union; p.52 *Source L* from *Racism: whose problem, whose decision?* published by the Scripture Union; p.57 *Source K* by Janet Morley, from the *SPCK Book of Christian Prayer*; p.69 *Source G* by John Bell, from the *SPCK Book of Christian Prayer*; pp.70–71 by permission of Christian Aid; p.77 *Source D* by Miriam Therese Winter, from the *SPCK Book of Christian Prayer*; p.80 from *What the Churches Say*, published by the Christian Education Movement; p.91 *Source J* © David Hare 1996; p.104 *Source J* by Caryl Mickelm, from the *SPCK Book of Christian Prayer*; p.115 *Source C* © David Hare 1996; p.123 from *I shall not be moved* by Maya Angelou, published by Virago.

Biblical quotations have been taken from the *Good News Bible*.

Photo acknowledgements
Cover Tony Morrison/South American Pictures; p.10 © Sonia Halliday Photographs; p.12 Popperfoto/Reuter; p.13 CC Studio/ Science Photo Library; p.15 *l* Paul Brown/Rex Features, *c* Chat Magazine/Rex Features, *r* K. Van Dyke/Lupe Cunha; p.17 Museo del Castello, Sforzesco/Bridgeman Art Library, London; p.18 *l* Popperfoto/Reuter, *r* © Sally & Richard Greenhill; p.20 *l* BFI Stills, Posters and Designs, *r* © Olivia Rayner; p.24 © Sharron Wallace/ St. Christopher's Hospice; p.25 *t* Rex Features, *b* © Miriam Reik/ Format; p.27 Popperfoto/Reuter; p.30 *l* Rex Features, *r* Simon Schluter/Rex Features; p.31 *t* Rex Features, *b* Borich/Rex Features; p.32 *tl* Petit Format/Nestle/Science Photo Library, *tr* Sally Lancaster/ Format, *b* SIPA/Rex Features; p.34 *tl* Steve Richards/Rex Features, *bl* Action Images, *r* Lupe Cunha; p.36 Ark Press; p.38 *l* © Melanie Friend/Format, *r* Rex Features; p.40 *t & b* Jane Wells; p.41 *t & b* Jane Wells; p.42 © Viv Quillin; p.45 © Gordon Rainsford/Gaze; p.47 *l* Ministry of Sound, *r* by permission of LGCM; p.49 © Karen Robinson/Format; p.50 Rex Features; p.51 *tl* © Sonia Halliday Photographs, *bl* Sheffield City Art Galleries/Bridgeman Art Library, London, *r* Index/Bridgeman Art Library, London; p.53 Adrian Brooks/Rex Features; p.54 Newham Recorder Newspaper;

p.56 *l* © Richard Watt, *r* Barry Batchelor/Press Association/ Topham; p.57 © Viv Quillin; p.58 *l* © Sally & Richard Greenhill, *r* Jim Belben; p.59 *tl* The Sun/Rex Features, *tr* Kuus/SIPA Press/Rex Features, *b* SIPA Press/Rex Features; p.60 *t* Rex Features, *b* SIPA Press/Rex Features; p.62 pencil drawing by Ajubel; p.64 Private Eye; p.66 © Minn Cooper; p.67 *l* Lefevre Gallery, London, *r* © Andrew Moore/Rex Features; p.68 John M. Templeton; p.69 David Williams/David Williams Picture Library; p.70 *l & r* Christian Aid/Harriet Logan/Network; p.72 *t & b* Zefa; p.73 Window designed by Tom McGuinness and crafted by stained glass artist Edna Partridge; p.74 Janet Orchard; p.75 *t, bl & br* Janet Orchard; p.76 Tapestry by Pamela Pavitt from 'Leaves from the Tree of Peace' © United Reformed Church 1986; p.77 *t* © Aislin/Cartoonists & Writers Syndicate, *bl* © Andrew Dunsmore/Rex Features, *br* © Mike Hutchings/SIPA Press/Rex Features; p.78 Adam Hart-Davies/ Science Photo Library; p.79 *t, bl & br* Janet Orchard; p.81 *tl* The Times/Rex Features, *tr* Scotsman Publications Ltd., *bl* Paul Brown/ Rex Features, *br* © Moir/Cartoonists & Writers Syndicate; p.82 Collection Imperial War Museum, London/© Janey Welsh; p.84 © Mike Wells/Aspect Picture Library; p.85 The Times/Rex Features; p.87 *t* OSPAAL, *b* Joanne O'Brien/Format; p.88 © Luke Warm; p.93 Space Telescope Science Institute/Science Photo Library; p.94 *t* Alan Olley/GMTV, *bl* Martin Dohrn/Science Photo Library, *br* Robert Harding Picture Library; p.97 Jim Belben; p.98 *l & r* John Rajah; p.99 John Rajah; p.101–2 *artwork l to r* Ellen Horner, Alison Ely, Hannah McSorley, Gemma Larkin, St Bede's Comprehensive Church School, Cambridge; p.105 *t* Santa Maria Novella. Florence/Bridgeman Art Library, London, *b* Reproduced by kind permission of The Dean and Chapter of Chichester (photo: John Crook); p.107 *l* The St. Louis Art Museum (Modern Art), Bequest of Curt Valentin 185:1955/© DACS 1998, *r* Tony Morrison/South American Pictures; p.110 © Sporting Pictures (UK) Ltd; p.111 Associated Press/Topham; p.112 Rex Features; p.113 *l* © Brenda Prince/Format, *r* Reproduced with permission of the Library Committee of the Religious Society of Friends in Britain; p.114 Popperfoto/Reuter; p.117 Musee d'Orsay, Paris/Bridgeman Art Library, London; p.119 Baptistry, Florence/Bridgeman Art Library, London; p.120 Tretyakov Gallery, Moscow/Bridgeman Art Library, London; p.121 *t & b* Sally Lynch; p.122 Palazzo Medici-Riccardi, Florence/Bridgeman Art Library, London; p.123 Andy Chambers/Rex Features; p.126 J. Kuus/SIPA Press/Rex Features; p.127 *t* Kunsthistorisches Museum, Vienna/Bridgeman Art Library, London, *c* Topham Picturepoint, *b* John Stillwell/Press Association/Topham.

t = top, *l* = left, *r* = right, *b* = bottom, *c* = centre.

While every effort has been made to contact copyright holders, the publishers apologise for any omissions, which they will be pleased to rectify at the earliest opportunity.

UNIT 1

How do Christians make moral decisions?

The characters in this cartoon are wrestling with the idea of religion.

Which character in this cartoon can you most relate to? Why?

How do you react to religion? How relevant do you think religious ideas are to the world today? Record your views at the beginning of this course. Later in this book, after you have explored how Christians apply their beliefs to some issues facing them in the modern world, you will see if your views have changed at all.

1.1   What would you do if …?

Morality is the study of right and wrong. To start thinking about how Christians make moral decisions, you are going to look at how *you* make them. Here are four everyday dilemmas. What do you think is right and wrong in these situations?

ACTIVITY A

Work in pairs. Consider each dilemma in turn.

1   **What do you think is the 'right' thing for the person to do in this situation? Explain why you think it is right.**
2   **What do you think is the 'wrong' thing? Explain why you think it is wrong.**
3   **Explain what you would do if you were in that situation.**
4   **List the factors that would affect your decision if you were in that situation.**
5   **When everyone has considered at least two dilemmas, make a class list of the factors that affected people's decisions.**
    a)   **Which are the most popular factors?**
    b)   **Why do you think they are the most common factors?**

Dilemma 1: The £10 note

I never have as much money as my friends. My mum is so tight with her money. I don't have as many clothes, CDs or treats as everyone else. They all go out more than I do and their parents always pay for them. One day I got home from school a bit earlier than usual. Mum was still at work. I noticed that she had left a £10 note in the kitchen. I thought of all the things that I could do with the money . . .

Should she:
Take the money
or
Leave it where it is
or
… ?

Dilemma 2: The lousy school report

I'm always getting into trouble at school. The teachers are always getting at me. The homework is too hard and takes too long. Other people get their parents to help them but my dad won't help me. I don't think he can do it either, but he won't admit it. I've got my end of year report in my bag to take home to my dad. It's really bad. He'll kill me when he reads it. I'm in trouble . . .

Should he:
Hide the report
or
Show the report to his dad
or
… ?

ACTIVITY B

I   Not all decisions are moral decisions. Do you think the following are moral decisions or not?
   a) what to have for breakfast
   b) who to choose as your boyfriend or girlfriend
   c) whether to shop at Safeway or Kwik-Save
   d) which football team to support
   e) whether to give money to Comic Relief
   f) whether to travel to school by car or bus
   g) whether to have an abortion.
   Give reasons for your answers.

SAVE AS ...

2   Keep a moral dilemma diary for a few days. Note down every time you face a moral dilemma – a situation where you feel you have to decide between right and wrong. Note possible courses of action, the decision you take, and why.

Dilemma 3: The new boyfriend

My family is very strict. As soon as school finishes I am expected to go straight home. One time a teacher kept me behind for a detention without telling my parents. My dad was furious. He came up to school and shouted at the people in the office. I felt really embarrassed.

Now I've met this boy I really like. Dad will say I'm too young to have a boyfriend so the only way I can meet him is to sneak out of school to meet him in the park. I've already been caught once. If it happens again they said they would tell my dad.

I don't know what my dad will do if he finds out . . .

Should she:
Give up her boyfriend
or
Keep on seeing her boyfriend in secret
or
. . . ?

Dilemma 4: Under-age drinking

There's this group in my class who go out at weekends and have a good time and get really drunk.

I get on OK with them and I've even been asked to go along. I'd like to, it would be great for my image, but I'm not sure I should. I don't think my parents would care. They go out themselves every Friday and Saturday. And I'm 15, almost an adult . . .

Should he:
Go out drinking with his friends
or
Find something else to do on Friday and Saturday nights
or
. . . ?

1.2 The Moral Ocean

✓. CHECKPOINT

You will need to know the meaning of these two terms:

- ABSOLUTE MORALITY – this is when a person believes that there is a right course of action in a moral dilemma that is true in all situations, regardless of culture, religious tradition, time or age. For example: 'it is always wrong to kill'.
- RELATIVE MORALITY – this is when a person has strong beliefs or principles but they believe that different courses of action might be needed in different situations. For example: 'it is usually wrong to kill, but sometimes it might be necessary for a particular reason.'

How do you decide between right and wrong?

- Do you ask advice from other people?
- Do you think of what your religion or upbringing has taught you?
- Do you work out an answer for yourself?
- Do you think, 'What would happen if I …' and go for the option with the best outcome?
- Do you think, 'What would so-and-so do in this situation?' and try to follow some example?
- Do you have a different way altogether?

This diagram shows some of the factors that might influence people when making moral decisions.

ACTIVITY

Making moral decisions is a bit like steering a ship through dangerous or exciting unknown waters. To help you reach a decision you are happy about and which you feel is right, there are 'islands' you can visit. These islands are your 'sources of moral authority'. What route would you take? What route would a Christian take?

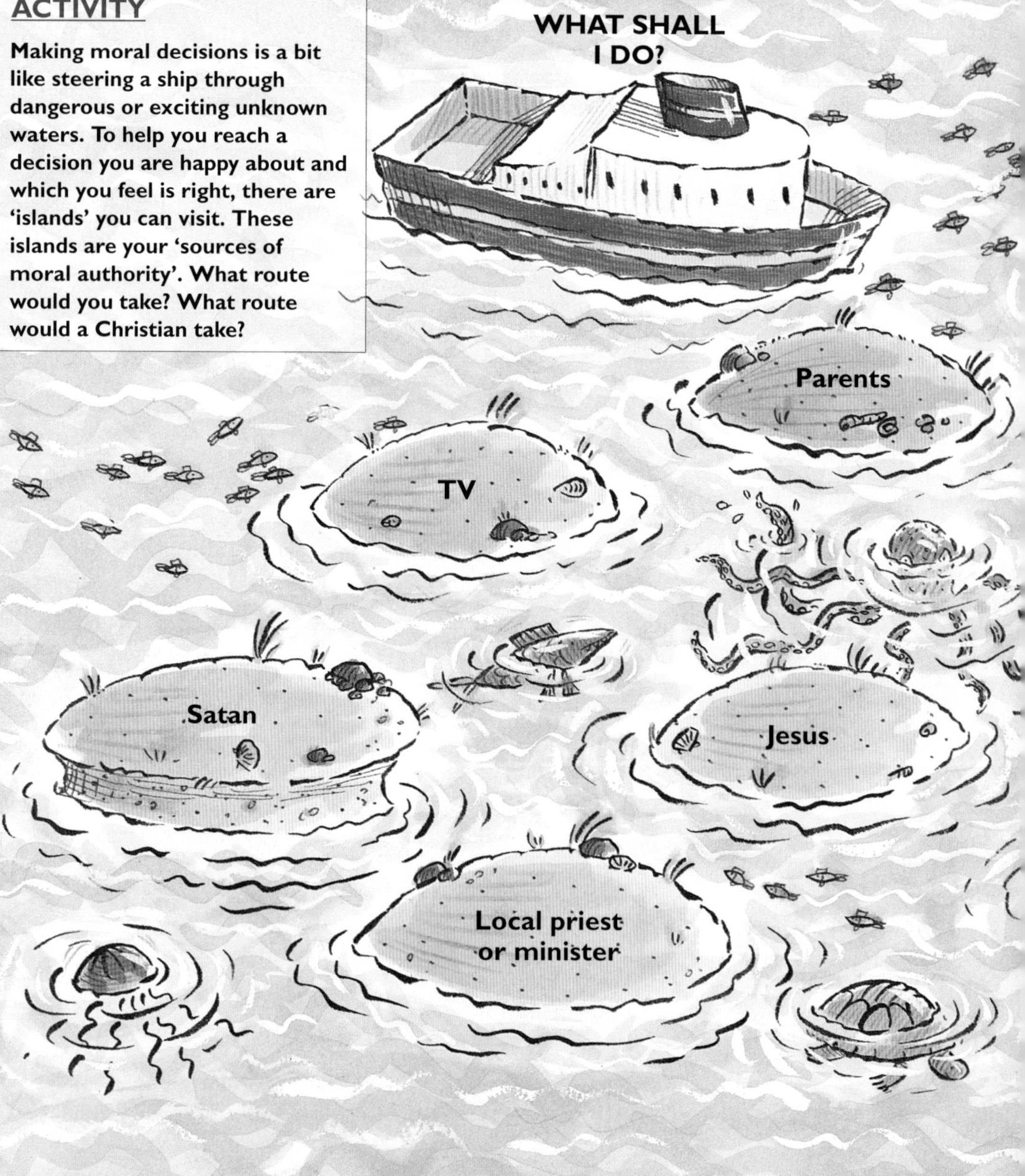

WHAT SHALL I DO?
Parents
TV
Satan
Jesus
Local priest or minister

SAVE AS…

Throughout this book you will be investigating examples of people who have taken absolutist or relativist stances. Draw up a table with three columns:

- **issue**
- **absolutist example(s)**
- **relativist example(s).**

As you work through this book you can use it to record examples of each approach.

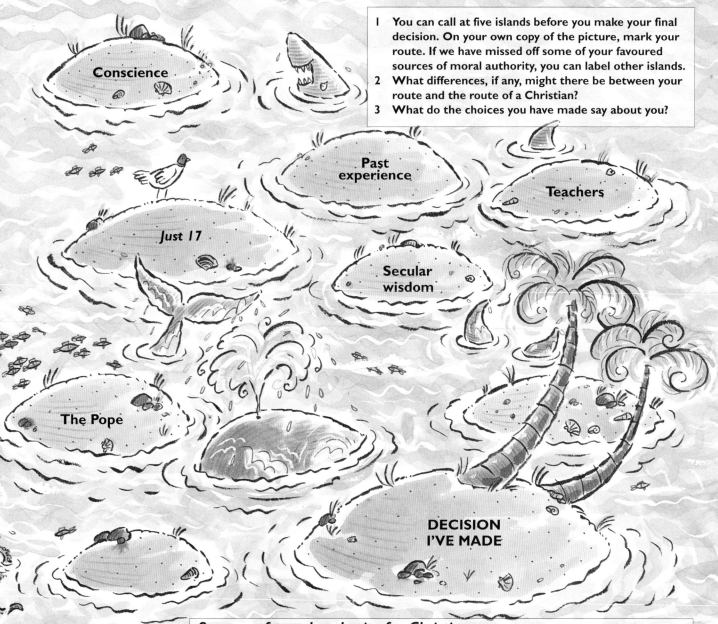

1 You can call at five islands before you make your final decision. On your own copy of the picture, mark your route. If we have missed off some of your favoured sources of moral authority, you can label other islands.
2 What differences, if any, might there be between your route and the route of a Christian?
3 What do the choices you have made say about you?

Conscience

Past experience

Teachers

Just 17

Secular wisdom

The Pope

DECISION I'VE MADE

The Bible

Sources of moral authority for Christians

Different Christian traditions favour different routes through the Moral Ocean. For example:

- Evangelical Christians emphasise that God's guidance can be found in the inspired words of *the Bible*.
- Catholic and Orthodox Christians emphasise how the *official teachings of their Church* can also guide Christians and they stress the role of *individual conscience* in making moral decisions.
- Many Christians from all traditions find that that their own *reason* and the *advice of other people*, such as Christian leaders, writers or friends can guide them.
- All Christian traditions see Jesus' life as a source of moral authority. Jesus is called 'the Word of God' by one of the New Testament writers. It is as if *Jesus' words and actions* show how God wants Christians to behave. Many Christians therefore ask: 'What would Jesus do in this situation?' and try to follow this example.

Through this course you will explore how different Christian traditions use these and other sources of moral authority in making moral decisions.

1.3 Christian traditions

Since the earliest days of Christianity, different traditions within Christianity have emphasised different aspects of faith. In this book we will be focusing in particular on studying the Catholic Church, and the Anglican Church as an example of a Protestant Church.

A

Christian traditions

1906 Pentecostal
1878 Salvation Army
1784 Methodists
1658 Presbyterians

The Protestant Churches themselves continued to split into different Churches, such as Baptist, Anglican, Methodist, etc., which are similar to each other but not identical.

Around 1500 a new movement within the Catholic Church called for the Church to change. The reformers wanted the Church to concentrate on Bible teaching and authority. They objected to the corruption in the Church and to the use of Latin, which they wanted to drop in favour of languages ordinary people spoke. This protest, now known as the Reformation, led to a split in the Church which was helped by political changes taking place at the time. The Protestant Churches split from the Catholic Church.

PROTESTANT

Over time the Orthodox Church split into different groups, such as Greek Orthodox, Russian Orthodox, etc.

Around 1050 the Christian Church split. The Eastern half developed into the Orthodox Church. The Western half developed into the Roman Catholic Church. As they developed in different places they included characteristics of different cultures. The Orthodox Church emphasised the mystery of God. The Catholic Church emphasised the authority of the Pope to speak on behalf of God.

ORTHODOX

CATHOLIC

Jesus was Jewish. Christianity grew out of Judaism, starting in about 33CE

✓ CHECKPOINT

Diversity

The diagram makes the divisions between the traditions, called 'Churches' *seem* very clear cut. But Christians do not always fit neatly into these categories. Christians are individual human beings who consider things from their own point of view. They seek personal guidance from God. They follow their own conscience. Some Christians are very sure of God, some go through periods of great doubt. Most find that their beliefs change over time; some move from one tradition to another, combining elements of each. What is more, as a world religion, Christianity varies from country to country.

So, avoid generalising when you answer questions about Christianity. Words like 'most' and 'some' are particularly important in your written answers to show you recognise the different Churches and the different opinions held by Christians.

ACTIVITY

1   **On your own copy of Source A add extra branches to show other Churches or traditions that you know of. Explain in your own words how they relate to the other traditions.**
2   **What do you think a Christian would see as:**
    a) the advantages
    b) the disadvantages
    of there being so many different 'branches' to Christianity?

Evangelicals and liberals

Take a slice through a branch and you see that within each Church you might find great differences between evangelicals and liberals.

Evangelicals believe that the Church needs to 'go back to basics'. They would regard the Bible as their starting point on almost any issue. They also believe that people become Christians through conversion – admitting they have sinned and asking God's forgiveness for their sins. The evangelical tradition is particularly strong in the Protestant Churches.

Liberals believe that the Church needs to evolve according to the challenges facing it. They would say that the Bible reveals aspects of God that we must apply to our own situation, but they don't expect a book like the Bible, written in another culture at another time, to have the answers to everyday problems. They are concerned with developing the spiritual side of people in different ways rather than in making people conform to a specific Christian mould or set of beliefs.

In a Protestant Church such as the Anglican Church you will often find great differences of opinion between evangelicals and liberals. Many liberal Anglicans would find they have more in common with liberals in another Church than with evangelicals within their own Church.

B

6% Other
2% Methodist
3% Presbyterian
3% Anglican
4% Baptist
5% Lutheran
7% Pentecostal

5% Other
9% Orthodox
30% Protestant
56% Catholic

The proportion of world Christians that belong to each tradition

C

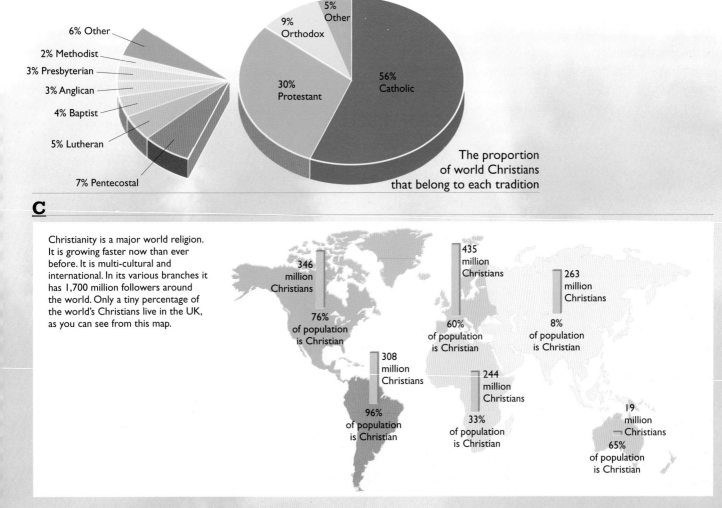

Christianity is a major world religion. It is growing faster now than ever before. It is multi-cultural and international. In its various branches it has 1,700 million followers around the world. Only a tiny percentage of the world's Christians live in the UK, as you can see from this map.

346 million Christians
76% of population is Christian

435 million Christians
60% of population is Christian

263 million Christians
8% of population is Christian

308 million Christians
96% of population is Christian

244 million Christians
33% of population is Christian

19 million Christians
65% of population is Christian

1.4   A Christian world view

Beliefs, values and behaviour

If you saw someone driving recklessly, you might think that they did not value other people's lives very highly. If you saw another person helping raise money for cancer relief, you might think the opposite. By observing how someone behaves you can tell a lot about their beliefs and values, because beliefs, values and behaviour are inter-related – they affect one another (see Source A). In this course, you will study how Christian beliefs and values are reflected in the moral decisions Christians take.

Some people say that if the human race wants to survive beyond the 21st century without destroying the Earth and everyone who lives on it, we need to rediscover the ability to make decisions based on clear moral values. They argue that the survival of the human race and of the planet depends on our recognising the difference between right and wrong.

This book is about how we make those difficult decisions and how the Christian religion can help us.

1   Should religious beliefs affect behaviour more than other beliefs?
2   Are Christians hypocritical if their behaviour is not affected by their Christian beliefs? Explain your answer.

A

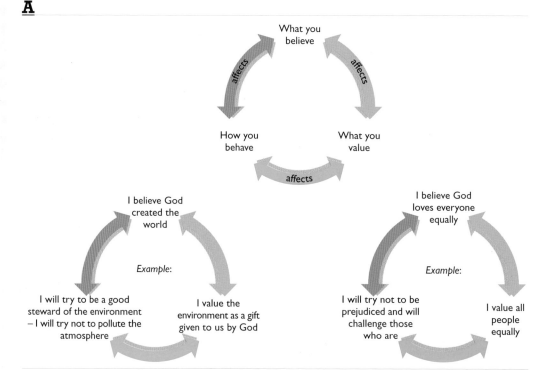

What do Christians believe?

Source B summarises some core Christian beliefs.

This is not a summary of all Christian beliefs – simply some of those beliefs about God, the world and human beings that most affect moral decisions. It will be clear to you from the previous page that it would be impossible to summarise Christianity in a way that satisfied all the different Christian traditions. However, most would agree with the beliefs in Source B at some level.

As you study Christian beliefs through this course you will regularly compare them with your own. You will decide how far Christian beliefs are useful in helping you make moral decisions in the world today. So, first things first, what do you think of these beliefs?

FOCUS TASK

Work in pairs.
1 Write each statement from Source B on a separate small slip of paper and place them all on a large sheet of paper.
2 You are now going to arrange these statements on the sheet according to how much you and your partner agree with them.
   a) Place near the centre of the sheet anything you both agree with.
   b) Place on your side of the sheet anything you agree with but your partner does not.
   c) Remove from the sheet anything neither of you agrees with. For every statement you get rid of, write another on the same topic that you can agree about!
3 Explain to what extent you agree or disagree with these core Christian beliefs.
4 Choose one belief and explain, using a diagram like Source A, how it might affect a Christian's values or behaviour.

B

God created the Earth and cares about it and the people who live on it.

In the end God will sort out all the mess in this world, with or without the help of humans.

When God made the Earth it was good. But people have spoilt it.

Individuals should not be separate islands. They are drawn together as partners, as community, as the Church.

God gives people free will. Many reject God's ways. Suffering and unhappiness are the result.

Each individual is unique and cared for by God. A person's life is holy and sacred.

Jesus shows what God is like and how we should live. Jesus' message of love and forgiveness can guide anyone back to God, and can overcome many of the problems human selfishness has created.

A moral code

Life would be almost impossible if every moral decision required Christians to go back to the Bible or to their Church leaders to work out a course of action. In practice, many moral decisions are simple for Christians because they have a moral code which serves as a handy guide to moral action. From early childhood, parents, schools and churches teach about right and wrong. These moral codes become so much a part of Christians' everyday life that they are hardly aware of them, yet they influence their behaviour. These codes allow Christians to follow what they feel is the right path without having to think hard about it.

The most famous part of the Christian moral code is the 'Ten Commandments', originally given to the Israelites more than 3,000 years ago, but still widely respected and used today (see Source C). These reflect some of the central beliefs and values of Christianity.

Jesus summarised these Commandments in two sentences (see Source D). He taught that love was more important than keeping laws and that if you live this way then you will reflect God's values in your life.

Another of Jesus' sayings has become known as the Golden Rule, since it is the simplest guide to moral decision-making (see Source E).

C

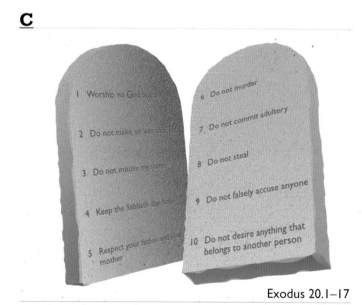

1 Worship no God but me

2 Do not make, or worship...

3 Do not misuse my name

4 Keep the Sabbath day holy

5 Respect your father and your mother

6 Do not murder

7 Do not commit adultery

8 Do not steal

9 Do not falsely accuse anyone

10 Do not desire anything that belongs to another person

Exodus 20.1–17

D

Love the Lord your God with all your heart, with all your soul, and with all your mind. Love your neighbour as you love yourself.

Jesus, in Matthew 22.37, 39

E

The Golden Rule

Do to others what you want them to do for you.

Jesus, in Matthew 7.12

F

Don't murder	87%
Don't drink and drive	79%
Don't steal	73%
Treat others as you'd like to be treated yourself	71%
Don't be violent	70%
Don't be racist	68%
Care for the environment	64%
Don't take drugs	60%
Be loyal to your friends	55%
Don't commit adultery	53%

0   50   100%

This is a new set of Ten Commandments agreed by teenagers in a recent survey. They were given the original Ten Commandments and a number of others to choose from. The graph shows the percentage of people surveyed who wanted each commandment in their moral code.

ACTIVITY A

Conduct your own research in class to see how people's ideas compare with Source F. You can get a survey sheet from your teacher.

ACTIVITY B

Hold a class debate on the motion: 'This house believes it is impossible to live today without a moral code.'

UNIT 2

Issues of life and death

Christians believe that life is a gift from God who is the Creator, the source of all life. But in today's society human beings seem to have greater power over life and death than ever before. Scientists can create life where there would have been none in the past. There seem to be more opportunities for ordinary people to make choices about life and death. For example, 40 years ago abortion was illegal in Britain. Now it is legal. A decision that used to be taken for you is now made by the individual. In some parts of the world, it is now possible for doctors legally to end a person's life, at their request. Christians would say that making something legal does not make it morally acceptable.

Is it right for human beings to make such decisions? If so, how do we make decisions about life and death?

2.1 The sanctity of life

'The fate of the frozen embryos'

These newspaper headlines come from a two-week period in the summer of 1996. Three thousand frozen embryos were to be destroyed.

A

Embryos are 'not people'

Childless families hope for eleventh-hour embryo reprieve

GOVERNMENT'S LAW OFFICER RULES THAT HUMAN EMBRYOS HAVE NO LEGAL RIGHTS

Catholic Cardinal demands respectful burials

Pro-Life group fails to halt destruction of embryos

B

The bizarre prospect of so many surplus embryos being created and then destroyed betrays the moral bankruptcy of our society in denying the intrinsic value of all human life.

Cardinal Basil Hume, leader of the Catholic Church in Britain, in a letter to the *Independent* newspaper

Why were these embryos frozen in the first place? IVF (in vitro fertilisation) involves doctors fertilising a woman's eggs with a man's sperm in a test tube. The resulting embryo is put in the mother's womb to grow. However, doctors might need many attempts before an embryo actually implants. They therefore freeze embryos for future use.

So why were they now being destroyed? The frozen embryos belong to the couple but, according to a law passed in 1991, they cannot be stored for more than five years without the permission of the couple. 1996 was the fifth anniversary of the new law so clinics all over the country contacted embryo owners to see if they wanted the clinic to keep or destroy the embryos. Many couples had lost contact with their clinic or their records were out of date, so on 2 August 1996 3,000 frozen embryos were due to be destroyed.

Who objected? The Catholic Church led a campaign against the thawing; it thought each embryo had a God-given right to life, that life should be preserved at all costs. It called on Catholic couples to offer to adopt the frozen embryos and for the woman to have an embryo implanted in her own womb. The Church claimed that 130 couples had volunteered.

Other protesters went to court to force the Official Solicitor, who has a legal duty to protect the interests of children, to save these embryos. He refused to intervene: 'I can only act on behalf of a life in being. Until a child is delivered it does not have an independent legal persona'.

Why such a fuss? There was more to this controversy than meets the eye. The argument was not just about these frozen embryos. As Source B explains, it was part of a much wider debate among Christians about how to react to the rapid development of embryo research.

Some Christians argue that embryologists are 'playing God'. In creating embryos at all they are behaving unethically. Other Christians welcome such developments because they can help give childless couples a child, yet they still worry about where all this will lead and want to ensure that such research does not devalue human life.

Does a frozen embryo have a right to life?

Christians say that life is sacred, but they do not agree about how to apply this belief to frozen embryos.

C

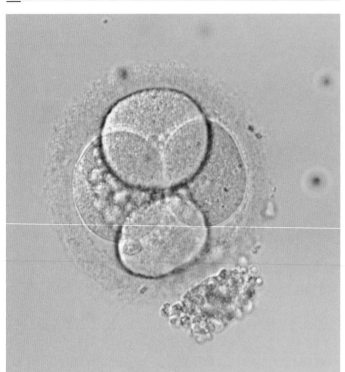

Magnified image of a human embryo 60 hours after conception. At this stage it has about four cells. An embryo cannot live on its own. To live, it would need to be implanted in a womb. Even if it was implanted in a womb there would be a high risk that the embryo would die.

D

From the time that the egg is fertilised, a life has begun which is neither that of the father nor of the mother. It is rather the life of a new human being with all its own growth. It would never be made human if it were not already human.

From the Catholic Declaration on Procured Abortion, 1974

E

… at this earliest stage of their existence, embryos do not have the moral value of persons. They are to be treated with respect; but essentially they are no different from the product of early miscarriages, and the way these have usually been handled is the best guide to what to do.

Lord Habgood, former Anglican Archbishop of York

1 **Which view do you most agree with: Source D or E? Explain why.**
2 **Explain why it is possible for Christians to take different views on this issue.**

What happened in the end?

There was no reprieve. The law was upheld. On 2 August 1996, 33 clinics began to thaw out the embryos. They broke down the cells with alcohol or salt solution and then incinerated them.

A doctor at one clinic said, 'It has been very distressing and frustrating for everyone.'

Another said, 'Of course one is not happy about destroying them, but the law is quite clear and it has to be done.'

ACTIVITY

1 **A local radio chat show is holding a phone-in on the issues raised by the case of the frozen embryos.**
   As a class, run the phone-in. Your teacher might act as the radio presenter. Each of you should 'ring in' to state your view or make a comment and give your reasons for whether the embryos should have been saved.
2 **Choose one of the headlines in Source A and, using the information on these two pages, write a brief article which could appear in a religious newspaper under that headline. You should include:**
   • **what the debate was about and why it aroused such controversy**
   • **what the Churches said about it**
   • **your own point of view.**

All life is sacred ... a Christian principle

Most people feel that life is valuable. But Christianity teaches that every person is made in God's image and all life is a gift from God and is therefore sacred. Source F summarises the main ideas:

FOCUS TASK

1   Make your own copy of the diagram in Source F.
2   Look up the following passages in a Bible. These are passages that some Christians would use to support the ideas in Source F.

> Psalm 139.13–16   1 Corinthians 3.16–17
> Genesis 1.27   Exodus 20.13
> Luke 12.6–7

3   Write each Bible reference alongside the idea which it supports. Add your explanation of *how* it supports this idea. You might feel some of the passages can be used to support more than one idea.
4   Across the bottom of your diagram write your own short caption summarising what Christians mean by 'the sanctity of life'.
5   Use your finished diagram and caption to create a poster called 'The sanctity of life'.

F

Key questions for Christians

The sanctity of life is a core principle for Christians. However, as the case of the frozen embryos shows, applying that principle in the real world raises difficult questions. The dilemmas are summarised in Source G.

✓ CHECKPOINT

You will need to know the meaning of the term SANCTITY OF LIFE. This is the belief that life is holy or sacred. You will need to be able to understand how Christians apply it to different moral issues. It reappears in the investigations into abortion (2.2), euthanasia (2.3), capital punishment (2.4), the environment (4.3) and war and peace (4.4).

G

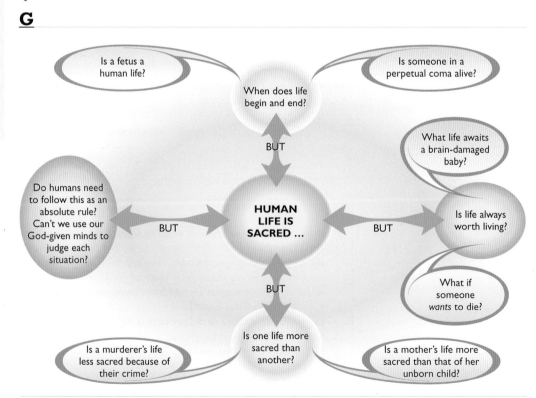

2.2 Why do many Christians oppose abortion?

When is abortion legal in Britain?

Before 1968 abortion was illegal in Britain.

Since the 1968 Abortion Act abortion has been legal in Britain if:
- two doctors agree that it is needed
- it is carried out on registered premises
- the baby is not yet capable of surviving. (The legal term used is 'viable' – this means 'able to survive apart from the mother if born and cared for medically').

In deciding if an abortion is needed, doctors must consider whether:
- the life, health or mental health of the mother is at risk
- an existing family will suffer if the pregnancy continues
- there is a reasonable chance that the child will be born handicapped.

In 1968 the latest termination date in cases of risk to the mother's mental health or an existing family was set at 28 weeks. In 1990 this was reduced to 24 weeks. There is now no time limit in cases of risk to the mother's life or health or of the baby being handicapped.

The number of abortions has risen steadily (see Source A).

In practice 'the mental health of the mother' has been interpreted to include distress that the mother might feel regarding pregnancy or motherhood. Some people say that in Britain there is effectively 'abortion on demand'. Some would even say that abortion is now treated as a form of contraception.

The law allows medical staff to abstain from performing abortions. However, some who have tried to opt out have found their jobs at risk.

Sammi is 16 years old, about to start her GCSE year, and has just discovered that she is seven weeks pregnant.

Ms X is in her twenties. She is ten weeks pregnant with twins. The twins are healthy but she already has one child. She is not married to her partner and does not feel able to raise two more children. She would like just one more child. She is considering 'selective abortion'. Doctors can inject one fetus to kill it. This endangers the life of both babies, but if it succeeds the dead fetus shrivels up and the remains are born with the placenta at full term.

Mrs Oldfield is in her thirties. Her husband has just left her for another woman and moved abroad. She is left with two children under ten years of age. To her surprise, she finds she is 12 weeks pregnant with her estranged husband's baby.

Mrs Perry is in her thirties. She is a practising Christian. She is pregnant with her first child and has just been told that a scan has shown that her 22-week-old fetus is almost certain to be born with a severe physical handicap.

ACTIVITY

1 Work in small groups. For each of the four case studies discuss:
  a) What action should the person take immediately?
  b) What factors should influence the person's decision as to whether to ask for an abortion?
  c) Should each person be allowed an abortion?
  d) What support or help will the person need?

2 Look again at the case of **Ms X**. This is a real case, which caused a storm of protest when the story appeared in the press. Do you think that aborting one twin is morally different from:
  a) aborting a single fetus as in the first three case studies
  b) aborting both twins?
  Give your reasons.

SAVE AS . . .

3 Write a letter to one of the women, telling her your views on her situation and what you would advise her to do.

Key questions for Christians

- When does life begin?
- Does a fetus have a God-given right to life?
- Who has the right to choose whether a fetus lives or dies?
- Should people have free will to make such decisions?

When does life begin?

A

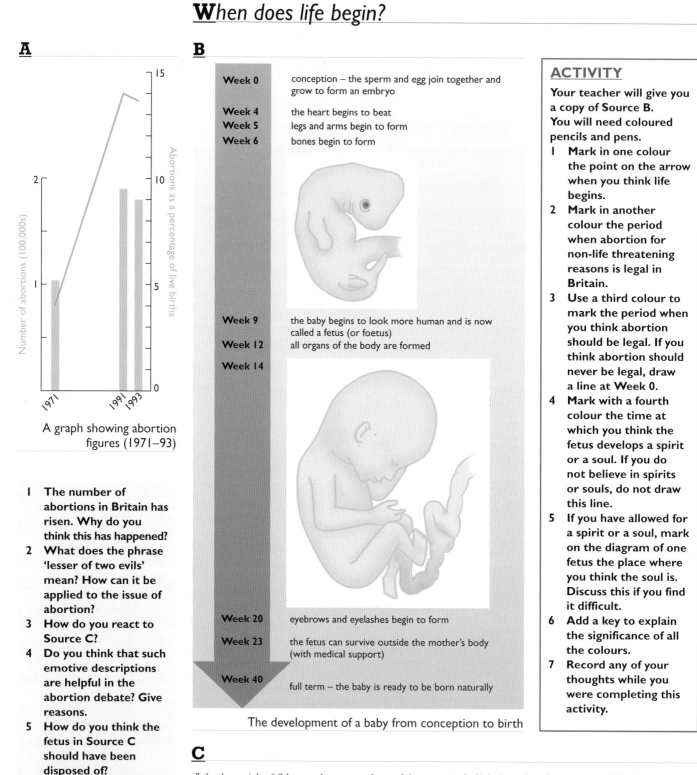

A graph showing abortion figures (1971–93)

1 The number of abortions in Britain has risen. Why do you think this has happened?
2 What does the phrase 'lesser of two evils' mean? How can it be applied to the issue of abortion?
3 How do you react to Source C?
4 Do you think that such emotive descriptions are helpful in the abortion debate? Give reasons.
5 How do you think the fetus in Source C should have been disposed of?
6 How do you think Christians who supported the introduction of the Abortion Act feel in the light of the statistics in Source A?

B

Week 0	conception – the sperm and egg join together and grow to form an embryo
Week 4	the heart begins to beat
Week 5	legs and arms begin to form
Week 6	bones begin to form
Week 9	the baby begins to look more human and is now called a fetus (or foetus)
Week 12	all organs of the body are formed
Week 14	
Week 20	eyebrows and eyelashes begin to form
Week 23	the fetus can survive outside the mother's body (with medical support)
Week 40	full term – the baby is ready to be born naturally

The development of a baby from conception to birth

ACTIVITY

Your teacher will give you a copy of Source B.
You will need coloured pencils and pens.
1 Mark in one colour the point on the arrow when you think life begins.
2 Mark in another colour the period when abortion for non-life threatening reasons is legal in Britain.
3 Use a third colour to mark the period when you think abortion should be legal. If you think abortion should never be legal, draw a line at Week 0.
4 Mark with a fourth colour the time at which you think the fetus develops a spirit or a soul. If you do not believe in spirits or souls, do not draw this line.
5 If you have allowed for a spirit or a soul, mark on the diagram of one fetus the place where you think the soul is. Discuss this if you find it difficult.
6 Add a key to explain the significance of all the colours.
7 Record any of your thoughts while you were completing this activity.

C

A baby girl of 21 weeks was placed in a metal dish in a back room and left to die after a hospital abortion, it was alleged last night. It was said to have taken three hours. A doctor said that it was pointless trying to save the child and she was finally wrapped in a plastic bag and put into the incinerator at Carlisle's City General Hospital. One nurse who took part in the operation was so distressed that she carried out her own form of baptism.

Daily Mail, 8 February 1988

What does Christianity teach about abortion?

Abortion is not mentioned in the Bible, but from its earliest history the Church consistently opposed it (see Sources D and E). This remained the attitude of most Christians until the 1960s.

D

Thou shalt not slay thy child by causing abortion, nor kill that which is already born, for everything that has been shaped by and has received a soul from God, if it is slain, shall be avenged.

From the *Apostolic Constitution*, written in the fourth century CE

E

Abortion is worse than killing a man in his own home.

John Calvin, a leading Protestant theologian, 1509–64

Pro-choice

In the 1960s many old ideas were reconsidered. Some Church leaders felt that traditional teaching on abortion was not useful in the modern world because dangerous, illegal abortions were being carried out in unhealthy conditions, by unqualified people, at great risk to the mother's health. There were between 40,000 and 200,000 illegal abortions each year. About 30 women died from illegal abortions each year. Some Christians argued that the most moral thing to do was to resolve this situation. They felt that legalised abortion was the lesser of two evils. David Steel, the MP who introduced the Abortion Bill to Parliament, was himself a Christian.

These Christians did not reject the idea of sanctity of life, but they weighed it against other principles from the Bible. They considered that abortion might be permissible in some circumstances.

F

The Bible's command is to love one another and to have compassion for the weak. I suggest that the most loving thing in many cases may be to allow the unsupported, single mother to have an abortion.

Jesus invites us to live a full life. What kind of life awaits a severely brain-damaged fetus?

God gives us free will. Who are we to take it away from someone?

Arguments used by Christians who take a pro-choice stance towards abortion

Pro-choice Christians leave it to individuals to decide whether abortion is right or wrong for them. They feel it is impossible to make rules that apply in all situations, and that individuals are best placed to make difficult moral decisions such as whether to have an abortion.

To be pro-choice does not mean to be pro-abortion. Many pro-choice Christians would see abortion as a last resort. They tolerate abortion rather than favouring it.

Pro-life or anti-abortion

Other Christians maintained and defended the Church's traditional teaching on abortion. In 1968 Pope Paul VI published his authoritative statement *Humanae Vitae* ('On Human Life'). It restated as an absolute rule for all Catholics that abortion was wrong.

G

Abortion has been considered to be murder since the first centuries of the Church, and nothing permits it to be considered otherwise.

Pope Paul VI speaking in 1970

Many evangelical Protestants are also supporters of the pro-life stance.

7 Record these examples of absolutist and relativist morality in the chart you began on page 4.

Compassion

Many Christians would feel it was important to show compassion for the woman, whatever her decision. This would mean showing that they cared for her and would support her whether or not they agreed with her actions.

Christian views on abortion

Abortion remains an emotive issue. There are Christians who hold strong pro-life views and those who are strongly pro-choice.

H

Abortion is always a tragedy, both in the life which is destroyed and in the health of the mother. It should never be used as a method of birth control. Those women who do have abortions need to be offered care and compassion.

TEAR Fund population policy. TEAR Fund is an evangelical agency working in developing countries.

ACTIVITY A

Sources H–O give a range of Christian responses to abortion.

1 **Make a copy of this scale. Write the letter of each Source in an appropriate place on your scale. Explain why you placed each one where you did.**

| strong pro-life | moderate pro-life | moderate pro-choice | strong pro-choice |

2 **Where would you put yourself on this scale? Explain your position.**
3 **List the different arguments for and against abortion which are used in the Sources.**
4 **List the alternatives to abortion which are proposed. Can you think of any others?**
5 **Which Source do you think takes the most loving or compassionate approach?**

I

'Have the baby,' they say. 'Someone will help you.' But where is the support when the mother has a screaming two-year-old, no money and feels like she hasn't a friend in the world. Motherhood is a lifelong commitment – a life of denying yourself and putting your child first – not to be entered into lightly.

Adoption is no cosy alternative. It is deeply traumatic for the mother and the child.

A Christian who works in fostering and adoption

J

A pro-life demonstrator protests against President Clinton's policy on abortion, Washington, USA, 1997

K

Are we sure, on biblical grounds, that it is always the just and loving thing to bring into this demanding, complex world a badly deformed, perhaps even mentally incomplete individual? ... While the scriptures establish the sanctity of life, the stress of scripture is on the quality of life.

L. Kalland in *Abortion, Can an Evangelical Consensus be Found?*

L

Contraceptives will fail and humans make mistakes. There will always be unplanned pregnancies. But there are many couples longing to adopt. And there are many women and young girls who've gone ahead and had babies and found it wasn't the end of the world. There is help available, a baby is not the end of life but the beginning.

Victoria Gillick, a Catholic, writing in the *TV Times*, November 1990

M

In July 1997 the first baby was born to a 15-year-old mother under a new scheme started by the Catholic Church in Scotland. Mothers who choose to have their baby rather than an abortion receive money for clothes and equipment.

The scheme was set up in March 1997. It gets two enquiries per day from mothers who are deciding between abortion and continuing their pregnancy. The scheme is modelled on similar schemes operated for many years by the Society for the Protection of the Unborn Child.

N

Pro-choice demonstrators in 1989 protesting against the reduction of the termination date, which became law in 1990

O

The greatest destroyer of peace in the world today is abortion. If a mother can kill her own child, what is there to stop you and me from killing each other? The only one who has the right to take life is the One who created it.

It is only our hearts that are not big enough to want [these children] and accept them … If there is a child you don't want or can't feed or educate, give that child to me. I will not refuse any child.

We are fighting abortion by adoption and have given thousands of children to caring families. And it is so beautiful to see the love and unity a child brings to a family. The child is the most beautiful gift of God to a family, to a nation. Let us never refuse this gift of God.

Catholic Mother Teresa in a letter to the UN Population Conference, 1994

1 Explain how each of the following religious principles is relevant to abortion:
   a) sanctity of life
   b) quality of life
   c) compassion
   d) free will.
   Use examples from Sources H–O to support your explanations.
2 Supporters and opponents of abortion use very different language to describe the unborn fetus. Find examples in Sources C–O and explain why they use these different terms.

ACTIVITY B

Look at this unfinished story strip. Your task is to complete two versions of it. The first should show how the story might finish if the advice centre Sammi goes to is run by pro-life Christians. The other should show how it might end if it is run by pro-choice Christians. Remember that pro-life Christians take an absolutist stance that abortion is wrong, although they cannot force anyone to take their advice. The pro-choice Christians take a relativist stance, according to the circumstances of the mother-to-be. Try to incorporate as many of the ideas on pages 15–19 as you can.

FOCUS TASK

Write an essay with the title 'Why do many Christians oppose abortion?' You may want to structure your essay by writing in paragraphs as follows:

* Abortion is …
* Some Christians oppose abortion because …
* Others disagree with them and prefer to leave individuals to decide because …
* Both can base their beliefs on the Bible because …
* We learn from this that moral decisions for Christians are …
* My own view on the Christian viewpoints presented is … because …

2.3 Murder, mercy killing or gentle and easy death?

ACTIVITY

Sources A and B give different impressions of euthanasia.

1 Describe the impression each picture gives you.
2 Supporters of euthanasia often call it mercy killing. Opponents describe it as murder. The word 'euthanasia' actually means 'gentle and easy death.' Which term best fits the pictures?
3 Which term comes closest to your own view? Explain why.

B

An illustration from the *New Internationalist* magazine in 1997, illustrating a pro-euthanasia article

Euthanasia in Britain

Euthanasia is illegal in Britain. However, there have been a number of attempts to get a bill through Parliament legalising euthanasia. All have failed. One example was a bill in 1969. If it had been passed, it would have allowed euthanasia on request to anyone over 18, provided that: 'two doctors believed the patient to be suffering from a serious physical illness or impairment, reasonably thought in the patient's case to be incurable, and expected to cause considerable distress.'

A

A scene from a 1930s film called *I Accuse*. This was pro-euthanasia propaganda made by the Nazis. The wife is severely disabled by incurable multiple sclerosis. The husband is persuading her that it is in both their interests that she be killed.

Euthanasia guidelines in The Netherlands

- There must be persistent, informed and voluntary requests by a patient who is aware of all the alternative treatments.
- There must be relentless suffering.
- There must be an independent medical appraisal by at least one other doctor supporting the decision.
- After death, the doctor must complete an exhaustive questionnaire and inform the coroner, who will visit to view the body and to verify the facts. The Ministry of Justice decides on the basis of this report whether or not to prosecute the doctor.

What is euthanasia?

Euthanasia is ending a person's life deliberately, but for compassionate reasons. Euthanasia is illegal in Britain, but the Voluntary Euthanasia Society campaigns for the law to be changed to allow it within a strictly controlled legal framework. This is the situation in the Netherlands, where euthanasia remains illegal, but provided certain procedures are carefully followed, a doctor who administers euthanasia will not be prosecuted in the courts.

C

We have 20,000 requests for 'living wills' each year, showing that a large proportion of the British people would like to see voluntary euthanasia become legal. Using euthanasia would save scarce medical resources which could then be used to help those who can be cured, they say. Everyone should be able to have 'the mercy of a painless death'.

Richard Hume of EXIT, the Voluntary Euthanasia Society.
In a living will a person asks for euthanasia in the event that they become terminally ill and unable to communicate their own decision to relatives or doctors.

Key questions for Christians

- Does free will give someone the 'right to die'?
- What is the most compassionate response to someone who wants to die?
- How can Christians best care for the suffering and the terminally ill?
- How can you judge someone's quality of life?

D

My patients can be sure that I will not let them suffer unnecessarily alone. That is my goal and my duty as a doctor.

Having the option of euthanasia makes it possible to concentrate not on the anxieties of suffering but on what people really want to do before they are going to die – like reconciliation with family members, saying their goodbyes, making a last trip downtown or out of the country. It really takes care of the burden of potential suffering which hovers over their heads like a shadow.

Euthanasia is not just about ending someone's life, but about how a life ends.

Doctor Gerrit Kimsma, a Dutch doctor and teacher of medical ethics who has performed euthanasia six times

1 **In the Hippocratic oath taken by all doctors they swear to 'do everything possible to preserve and restore life and not to take it.'**

Do you think the Hippocratic oath should be changed today? Give reasons for your answer.

The careful death of José

The following is a true story which took place in the Netherlands.

José was 30 years old when she asked a doctor to end her life.

She had been diabetic since childhood. The diabetes had destroyed the nerve endings in her stomach, meaning that she could not digest any food. She had to be fed through a tube which pumped liquid food directly into her intestine. Even so, liquid would seep back into her stomach and she would often vomit violently. Her weight dropped from 70 kg to 42 kg.

Her doctors tried every imaginable alternative treatment but with no effect. Finally, she asked her hospital specialist for euthanasia. He was unwilling to grant it and prescribed anti-depressant drugs instead. She took these, but they made her dull and unresponsive.

That's when her local doctor, a frequent visitor, said he was willing to consider euthanasia.

'It was a kind of relief,' said her husband Ron. 'We discussed it frequently. We both cried buckets of tears. We had a very open and honest relationship, but in the last few months the relationship went sky-high emotionally.'

Their doctor consulted a doctor appointed by the courts, and an independent doctor who gave a second opinion. A psychiatrist had to confirm José was in sound mind. Even then they had to wait four months before being 'approved' for euthanasia.

When the time came, José had planned her funeral service. The euthanasia was arranged for 8.00 p.m. on a Monday. Ron describes her last few days:

José was amazingly cool. On Saturday she had her last visit from her parents. On Monday she rang up a few people just to make sure that she had heard their voices. She dressed up the way she wanted to be cremated and did her hair. We watched a few U2 videos – her favourite band.

I asked her, 'How does it feel that you are going to die?'

She said, 'It's very restful, it's very peaceful. I can't give you the answer, but it's a good feeling. I did my trip. I fought my fight.'

Around eight o'clock she said, 'Well, I think I want a coffee because it won't come back up now!' She was on the couch with her coffee and her cigarettes when the doctors came. Our doctor said he had expected to enter a room full of emotions and sadness with family crying. He said that the obvious acceptance and serenity made it easier for him.

The doctors finally checked there were no doubts. She said, 'Well, I'm ready.'

We spent a few moments alone. What do you say? 'Have a good trip'? I had to cry. That was the strange thing – she comforted me. She said, 'It's going to be all right!'

Finally we called the doctors, and with me holding her hand she was given a narcotic to make her sleepy and then the fatal drug.

Life continues, but everybody has their own little voice and José is part of mine. She agreed to watch over me and I still think of her every day. She is there in the simple things.

DISCUSS
1 **Do you find the death of José morally acceptable?**
2 **Do people in your class hold different opinions about José's euthanasia? If so, explain your point of view to someone who disagrees with you.**

Christian principles

The Bible says nothing explicit about euthanasia. However there are many Biblical and religious arguments that can be applied to this debate both for and against euthanasia.

E

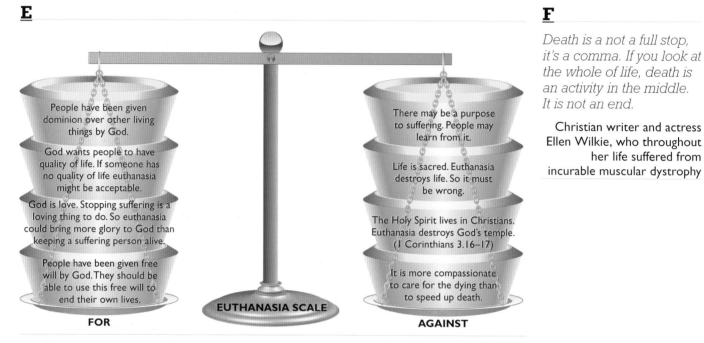

People have been given dominion over other living things by God.

God wants people to have quality of life. If someone has no quality of life euthanasia might be acceptable.

God is love. Stopping suffering is a loving thing to do. So euthanasia could bring more glory to God than keeping a suffering person alive.

People have been given free will by God. They should be able to use this free will to end their own lives.

FOR

There may be a purpose to suffering. People may learn from it.

Life is sacred. Euthanasia destroys life. So it must be wrong.

The Holy Spirit lives in Christians. Euthanasia destroys God's temple. (1 Corinthians 3.16–17)

It is more compassionate to care for the dying than to speed up death.

AGAINST

EUTHANASIA SCALE

F

Death is a not a full stop, it's a comma. If you look at the whole of life, death is an activity in the middle. It is not an end.

Christian writer and actress Ellen Wilkie, who throughout her life suffered from incurable muscular dystrophy

G

Instead of rules, we offer a process for working out the decision that is right for each person, in her or his circumstances.

Quaker guidance on euthanasia

H

No one has the right to bring about death by their own decision, whether by suicide or by voluntary euthanasia. Christians through the ages have found that the grace of God sustains heart and mind to the end in difficult situations and so can Christians today who face painful or drawn-out death.

Salvation Army guidance on euthanasia

I

The Catholic Church believes that euthanasia is wrong. Life is sacred. Only God can make decisions over death. The Pope said euthanasia was contributing to a 'profound change in the way life and relationships between people are considered' and called it 'a grave violation of the Law of God' (Encyclical, March 1995). Cardinal Basil Hume, Archbishop of Westminster, said he was '200 per cent' behind the Pope's teaching on this. He said in The Times, 31 March 1995, 'My plea is that society should stop and ask, where could all this lead?'

However, Catholics realise that in practice decisions on euthanasia are not straightforward. For example, Catholics accept that it is right to ease the suffering of the terminally ill, even when the effect of using pain-relieving drugs may be to end the patient's life sooner than if they were left to suffer. They do not see this as euthanasia, because no one is changing what would naturally happen in the situation.

A summary of Catholic teaching on euthanasia

1 **The arguments in Source E are not of equal weight. Which do you think should have the most weight? Which should have the least?**

2 **How far would a Christian agree with you?**

3 **Read Source F. Christians believe that there is life after death. On which side of Source E would you put this belief?**

4 **Compare Sources G–I. Which of these are examples of:**
   a) absolute morality
   b) relative morality?
   Record them on your chart.

5 **In Source G the Quakers refer to a process for making decisions. What do you think they mean?**

Should voluntary euthanasia be allowed in Britain?

This is a controversial issue. There is a strong lobby against euthanasia. There is also a strong lobby in favour of allowing voluntary euthanasia. In a recent confidential survey 18 per cent of Catholic doctors in the USA said they would administer euthanasia if requested by a terminally ill patient. In another survey one in eight Australian doctors admitted that they had helped someone to die at their request. British doctors have also admitted to helping the terminally ill to die. In the vast majority of cases doctors say they shortened the life of a terminally ill and suffering patient by only a matter of days.

FOCUS TASK A

You are going to have a class debate on the motion: 'This house believes that voluntary euthanasia should be allowed in Britain.'

To prepare for the debate:

1 **Study all the quotations on this page and divide them into arguments for and arguments against the motion.**
2 **In your book, finish these sentences, explaining clearly what you believe.**
   a) **I think euthanasia should be/not be made legal because …**
   b) **The strongest reason I have for saying this is …**

All life is sacred. Killing is always wrong. So euthanasia is wrong. It should never be legalised.

When I first had my accident I pleaded with the nurses and doctors to kill me, because I felt like dying. They did not and I am so thankful. Euthanasia would have robbed me of the chance to rediscover my human value – a value which is no less for the fact that I am still incurably disabled and suffering much pain. I think that euthanasia represents the ultimate 'hand-washing' exercise by a society which would rather kill than care.

Euthanasia is putting someone to sleep lovingly. Euthanasia can be an act of love. Love cannot be illegal.

What marks out humans from animals – you could call it our God-given ability – is that we have minds to think and reason things out.

We should not be scared of using our minds to decide if it is right to allow someone to die. Let's have a law which gives intelligent people responsibility for approving any request to die.

Anyone who knows about Nazi Germany could never support euthanasia. One thing leads to another. Euthanasia was the thin end of the wedge. The Nazis started by killing the mentally ill. They ended up slaughtering Jews by the millions.

Euthanasia misses the point. There is a point to suffering. We can learn from it. Christians should oppose the legalising of euthanasia.

It is impossible to make any euthanasia law that would work in all cases. It would be a nightmare. It all depends on the circumstances.

People change their minds. What if I write my living will, then after I'm too ill to talk or communicate, I regret it? Imagine someone coming to 'turn you off' and you can do nothing about it. No way.

FOCUS TASK B

After your debate, write an essay to explain whether you agree with the statement: 'A person has the right to end their own life when they wish.'

Explain your own view, showing that you have thought about and understood other viewpoints, including religious viewpoints.

The hospice movement: a Christian alternative to euthanasia

A hospice looks after people who are terminally ill. They are cared for by a wide range of trained medical staff. Their pain is relieved through drugs. Any fears about death that they or their families may have are talked about.

The first hospices were founded by Christians who were at the forefront in looking for compassionate alternatives to euthanasia.

J

I'm against euthanasia for a positive reason; I have seen people achieve so much in the ending of their lives – times that their families would have missed. It's often time after they might have asked to opt out when they perhaps would have gone in bitterness, whereas they finally go in peace and fulfilment.

Dame Cicely Saunders, a Christian, doctor and founder of the hospice movement

K

A visitor and resident in the chapel at St Christopher's hospice

M

I am so glad my mother came here to die. In the hospice she was cared for as a whole person, and my family and I were helped to deal with losing her. She had lived a long and happy life and I was very concerned that she should not leave this life in pain. The doctors and nurses helped her to manage her pain, and the Catholic priest was always there for us. My mother died peacefully in my arms with her family around her. That time in the hospice gave us the time to prepare for death and to tell her that we loved her. I had never been to a hospice before my mother went in, but now I work as a volunteer there to help and support other families.

David Stone

L

St Christopher's Hospice is:

- *a Christian foundation with staff and volunteers of many denominations or none*
- *a medical foundation, working to improve the quality of life remaining for people [with terminal illnesses]*
- *open to all who need its care, regardless of race, creed or ability to pay*
- *researching the support needed by dying patients and their families, in the hospice and at home*
- *a charity, built entirely with gifts and grants … funded by the generosity of friends and supporters.*

From an annual report of St Christopher's Hospice, South London, founded by Cicely Saunders (Source J) in the 1960s

1 **Suggest how a hospice volunteer, such as David Stone (Source M), might complete the following sentence. 'Dying naturally in a hospice is better than euthanasia because …'**
2 **Gerrit Kimsma (Source D) meets David Stone (Source M). In pairs, role play a conversation in which they discuss euthanasia.**

N

In every case, care is more merciful than killing.

The fatal tide of permissiveness is trying to persuade us that euthanasia – so clearly condemned as a criminal act and for centuries specially spurned in the Hippocratic oath – may now be acceptable, or even caring. Having spent two decades looking after patients dying in my general practice, I must disdain it as fundamentally wrong, entirely unnecessary when good practice takes place, and so widely open to abuse that it must continue to be highly unethical and illegal.

The strongest argument against euthanasia – apart from the moral one – is that there has never been greater ability to relieve pain and never more people professing to care for and cherish those in need. In our wealthy society there should be no need for termination of the sick.

A. Rogers, a Christian doctor, writing in the *Independent*, 12 May 1990

✓ CHECKPOINT
Quality of life
You will need to know what Christians mean by the phrase 'quality of life'. It is not a measure of material possessions or a comfortable life, but a measure of fulfilment. If a person feels right with God, right with others and right in themselves then they could have a good quality of life whatever their circumstances.

This idea is also important in answering questions on abortion (2.2).

3 **Look at Sources O and P. Who do you think has the best quality of life? Give reasons.**

4 **Now imagine that the woman in Source O has got an incurable disease which means she cannot move herself. She has been helped to the swimming pool by a servant who has put the drink in her hand for her to suck through a straw. Does this affect your answer to Question 3?**

5 **Now imagine the woman in Source P is about to be evicted from her flat. She has no home to go to. No family. No money. No friends. The woman in Source O has a loving family who come to visit her every day to keep her company. She can talk to them even though she cannot move. Does this affect your previous answer?**

6 **Invent some more information about either person that you think would affect their quality of life for better or worse.**

What is quality of life?

One of the most common arguments used to justify euthanasia is that the person has no 'quality of life'. Let's look at this in more detail.

How people judge quality of life

O

P

How the Bible judges quality of life

Jesus said, 'I have come that you might have life – life in all its fullness.' (John 10.10). From the rest of his teaching it is clear that he thought someone's quality of life was determined not by their possessions but by:

- their relationship with God
- their relationships with others
- the feeling of rightness in themselves.

You cannot therefore see quality of life. You cannot really measure it because it is about what you feel like inside.

FOCUS TASK

1 Finish this sentence in as many different ways as you wish: 'Quality of life is . . .'
2 Tick any statements which Christians might agree with.
3 Put a cross by any statements which Christians would reject.
4 Write a paragraph explaining how the idea of quality of life is relevant to decisions about:
   a) abortion
   b) euthanasia.
5 Create a 'Quality of life' poster to go with your 'Sanctity of life' poster from page 14.

2.4   Does it help to execute murderers?

A

> Teenagers abduct and murder young child

> Drunk driver kills pedestrian while three times over the legal limit

> Young woman steals five dresses from clothes shop

> Husband seriously injures wife in marriage row

> Six dead in terrorist blast

ACTIVITY

Some people think Britain should bring back the death penalty. What do you think?

In groups, discuss which, if any, of the crimes in Source A, you think would justify capital punishment. Explain why.

Are there other crimes not mentioned that people in your group think deserve the death penalty?

Record your views in a table. In the first column, list the crimes; in the second column, put a tick or cross to say whether or not you believe it deserves the death penalty; in the third column, give your reasons.

Why do we punish people?

Almost everyone agrees that people who have committed a crime should be punished in some way. Source B looks at some of the reasons they give.

B

Deterrence – to discourage the offender (and other potential offenders) from committing similar crimes

Protection – for the safety of society, individuals in it, and sometimes the offender themselves

Reform – to help the offender to become a 'better' person

Retribution – revenge for those who have been wronged

Reparation – to allow the criminal to 'pay' for what they have done and have their guilt wiped out so they can make a fresh start

Vindication – to show that the authority of the law is being upheld – to ensure that people respect the law

FOCUS TASK A

1   Explain whether capital punishment can help to achieve each of the stated aims of punishment in Source B and if so, how.
2   Can life imprisonment achieve these aims better than capital punishment?
3   Are you in favour of the death penalty? Give your reasons.
4   What factors most affect your attitude to capital punishment?

Key questions for Christians

- What reasons for punishment are acceptable to God?
- How do we balance punishment and forgiveness?
- Is a life for a life a biblical principle?

Christian principles

One core issue for Christians is the sanctity of life (see page 12). A murderer's life is no less sacred than the life of any other human being. According to Christians, God gives life and only God has the right to take it away. A Christian in favour of capital punishment must be sure that this is God's will. In deciding this, Christians are faced with conflicting advice. There is plenty in the Bible that is relevant to the debate about capital punishment.

An eye for an eye

Gordon Wilson

In 1987 a terrorist bomb exploded at a Remembrance Day parade in Enniskillen, Northern Ireland. Among those killed was a young nurse called Marie Wilson. Later that day, in front of TV cameras, her father Gordon (see photo), a committed Christian, said that he forgave her killers.

I   Why do you think he did this?

Rules for when to use and when not to use capital punishment are spelled out clearly in the Old Testament (see Exodus 21.12–26, for example). The underlying principle is 'an eye for an eye, a tooth for a tooth'. which means a life for a life; no more, no less! God is seen as a fair judge who wants the punishment to fit the crime. Some crimes that were considered serious enough to be punishable by death at that time would still be seen as serious crimes today (murder, for example), others would not (such as adultery and worshipping false gods).

In the Old Testament, capital punishment is seen to **deter**, **protect** and **vindicate**.

Forgive others

Jesus' teaching on punishment stands in contrast to both the more legalistic approach of the Old Testament and the brutality of Roman law, under which people were crucified for any crime against the Roman authorities. Jesus says, in Matthew 5.38–48, that the idea of 'an eye for an eye' is to be replaced by a new attitude of **love** and **forgiveness**. Again and again he shows himself concerned with **reform** rather than retribution. In John 8.1–11 he forgives a woman brought to him for 'stoning', telling her to sin no more. In one of the most famous parables he pictures the whole of heaven rejoicing over just one evil person who repents and turns to God. On many occasions he reminds his followers to look at their own failings before being too hard on others.

Today, Christian ideas about punishment are greatly influenced by Jesus' approach. Christians do not deny the need for punishment; rather, they support punishments that give the offender every chance to reform. Capital punishment clearly does not allow this; prison, community service, probation, counselling, therapy and education all might.

Many Christians would say that **deterrence**, **protection**, **retribution** and **vindication** all need to be balanced against **reform**, even in the case of murder. 'A life for a life' is not consistent with Jesus' teaching.

The ancient principle of ensuring the punishment fits the crime lives on, for example in having longer prison sentences for serious crimes than for more minor ones. However, even in this regard, many Christians today would want to take the circumstances of the offender into account. The principle is to make the punishment fit the offender as much as making it fit the crime.

FOCUS TASK B

I   List all the different arguments for and against capital punishment. Refer to Source B. Underline the religious arguments.

2   Draw the arguments on a pair of scales showing which way the balance falls for you.

Does capital punishment work?

Discussion of capital punishment often focuses less on morality and more on the practical issue: does it work? It is the ultimate **protection**, and it certainly highlights **retribution**. Public anger against murderers and terrorists is such that only the death penalty seems to offer sufficient revenge. However, there is little historical evidence that it **deters** others from offending. In the case of terrorism, capital punishment might even encourage offenders as it offers them martyrdom. In the current climate, it arguably undermines rather than upholds the law, since it highlights weaknesses in the justice system. The accuracy of a court's guilty verdict cannot be guaranteed, yet it is impossible to bring back an executed person.

Is life imprisonment a better punishment than hanging?

Since the abolition of hanging, the usual punishment for murder in Britain is life imprisonment.

Sue, Nasreen and Mary are serving life sentences for murder. To preserve confidentiality, the exact details of their crimes cannot be revealed, but before the abolition of capital punishment each of them could have been hanged. One almost certainly would have been. They started their sentences in the early 1990s, aged between 30 and 45. They may be released once each has served her tariff (minimum period set by the Home Secretary). This will be not before 2010, but even after release they would remain 'on licence' for life and could be recalled to prison.

We asked the three women:

- Do you think you had a fair trial?
- How do you feel about being in prison?
- Do you think capital punishment should be brought back?

Nasreen

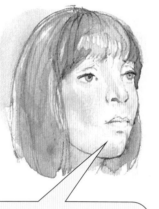

Sue

During my case people brought up things from my past which had nothing to do with the crime. I thought, 'Who are they talking about? – that's not me.' There was even a film about me on TV. It was so inaccurate. I think there should be laws preventing the press from publishing things about you from years ago.

The prison sentences are so long that we have no hope. I'll be 63 when I get out. Who will employ me then? I'm not even sure I could cope with the outside – here they take away our ability to think for ourselves. My prison could be real luxury, it could be Buckingham Palace, but it would still be prison, because they have taken me away from my family.

I think that capital punishment should be brought back for child-killers. In our cases there are circumstances that led to murder, but children have no past to make people want to kill them – they are innocent, there are no mitigating circumstances. And if you keep child-killers in prison, then what privileges should you give them? Do you lock them in their cell? It would be better to kill them. We don't have a bad life in prison – should they have that?

I agree with Sue. With all that was raked up at my trial, we are being punished for things that are nothing to do with the actual crimes. I feel angry; it's not fair on my family.

I am very unhappy in prison, though I have good days and bad days. I see prison as a way of satisfying society – people think it is good that we are here, and that the keys should be thrown away. I feel that the public treats us like animals. If we got out now we wouldn't be safe. If we get out, society will look on us as nothing because we have a record. You might as well die in prison.

I think that sentences in general are far too long and should be more individualised. Being in prison makes you think – it builds up remorse, so there should be a chance of release after, say, five years, if people really have changed. The sentence wears you down. There are times when I feel suicidal, but I wouldn't do it because of my kids. I cope with my punishment by seeing it as if I am punishing myself for all the things that I have done in the past. It's a bit like a test from God.

Prison is tough, but it will never change my personality. I study for exams that I didn't do when I was at school. What prison has done is to make me lose my faith in the media and the press.

I do not believe in capital punishment. I am a Christian and I believe that only God has the right to take life. Even child-killers shouldn't be killed, but they should be locked up for good. There are lots of really mentally sick people around and prisoners should be tested and then treated if necessary. Having said that, if anyone killed my kids I think I would kill them instantly, and then feel regret later.

Mary

I think that the law is unfair. Circumstantial evidence should not be used in trials – only tangible facts. It hurts that my character has been destroyed by all the lies at my trial. When I was outside I was very ignorant about prison life. I used to think that no one could be put in prison unless they were guilty.

Sometimes I feel very hurt and angry about being here, but I do not want to become bitter. Maybe God is preparing me for something. Who knows? I believe that I am here because I had to be educated. I was a typical 'good Christian' – doing all the right things, but maybe not for the right reasons. I've had time to look inside myself here. I have little hope for the future. I only want my daughter to be all right. I study; I am going to do a degree, and at the end of it all if I can stop one young person from ending up in here then it will be worth it.

I do not believe in capital punishment as it is so easy to make mistakes. I know someone in Africa who was shot by three men. He lived, but they were shot for attempted murder. When I heard about it I curled up inside – how do they know they have got the right men? In my experience the police tend to go for the easiest way to solve a case. If I was outside I would believe what I read in the papers and agree with hanging, but my experience in prison has taught me otherwise. My life is not my own to take anyway – God is around, I can feel him.

I think that the Church should have a say in ethical issues that affect society. The Bible gives examples of right and wrong. The Church should be screaming this from the rooftops. Many people actually need medical help rather than imprisonment.

DISCUSS

1 Read carefully what Sue, Nasreen and Mary say.
   a) Who do you think is the happiest?
   b) Who do you think is the most bitter about being in prison?
   Explain your answers.
2 The women disagree about capital punishment. How and why?
3 What do they see as the aim of their punishment?
4 All three were unhappy about their trials. Why?
5 During the interviews, all three women said they thought trial juries should be made up of trained people, rather than just ordinary members of the public. Do you agree?
6 Do you think that Sue, Nasreen and Mary have been dealt with fairly?
7 Do you think the fact that Nasreen and Mary are both Christians should affect the way they are treated? Explain why.
8 Do you think it is right for Christians to be involved in lobbying against the death penalty and for better conditions in prison?

<u>M</u>yra Hindley

One of the test cases of popular attitudes to life imprisonment is that of Myra Hindley. She and her lover Ian Brady tortured and murdered at least three children in the 1960s, when Hindley was still a teenager. The so-called Moors Murderers (they buried their victims' bodies on the Lancashire moors) were sentenced to life imprisonment on 6 May 1966 and Hindley has already served a much longer sentence than people with equivalent crimes. There was, and remains, a public revulsion to these crimes. Many people felt at the time that both should have been hanged. The crimes can still raise a massive debate, as you can see from Source C.

C

The subject of Myra Hindley's possible release on parole has been discussed many times and always provokes debate in the press. Many people feel she should remain locked up for ever. Other people, including Sue, Nasreen and Mary (see pages 28–9), think she should be released. What do you think?

In summer 1997, a painting of Myra Hindley made from children's hand-prints caused a massive protest when it was included in an art exhibition at the Royal Academy, London. The picture was immediately defaced by angry protesters who said it was exploiting Hindley's crimes and insulting the memory of the murdered children. The pressure group Mothers Against Murder and Aggression (MAMA) called for the picture to be immediately destroyed.

D

Her crimes were terrible crimes, but everyone who has assessed her agrees she is reformed and would not offend again if released. She's served the equivalent of a 50-year sentence with remission. Should we keep someone locked up for life just because the victims' families cannot forgive her?

A caller speaking on Radio 5 Live in summer 1997

Dignified death?

In some countries capital punishment is still used. In parts of the USA the death penalty was abolished but has since been brought back. There are currently about 3,000 people in the USA awaiting execution on Death Row.

Some see capital punishment as a way to get rid of what they call the 'maggots' that infest decaying American society. They believe it is the ultimate protection – an executed killer cannot kill again. They argue that it is cheaper than keeping someone in prison. There is also support among some American Christians for the death penalty.

Others have waged a vigorous campaign against it, saying it is not only anti-Christian and uncivilised, but also unfair and racist. For example, black murderers are much more likely to be executed than white murderers.

Opponents also argue that death by capital punishment is degrading: for the person being executed it is a humiliating, undignified death; for the witnesses who have to watch, for the media who report and for the public, executions are a ghoulish spectacle which bring out the worst in human nature.

1 How do you react to Sources E, F and G?
2 Do you think John Spenkelink died a dignified death?
3 Public executions used to be very popular entertainment. Executions today attract a lot of attention even though they are no longer public (although there must be independent witnesses). How do you explain this interest?
4 How should a Christian respond to the media interest an execution arouses?
5 How could a prison chaplain have tried to help John Spenkelink in the hours before his death?
6 How do you think a chaplain might feel about the death penalty?

E

Death Row and the electric chair in two US prisons

F

Just after ten o'clock John Spenkelink was wrestled from his cell by six guards and carried struggling down the hall. He was gagged because he had shouted, 'This is murder!' In the centre of the small room where he was taken was the electric chair.

Spenkelink was strapped into the chair at the arms, legs and chest. His mouth and chin were muzzled. A towel secured his head to the back of the chair. The guards put a wet sponge on his head to conduct electricity better. Two electrical wires were connected to his body. He caught a brief glimpse of the witnesses behind the glass before the hood was dropped quickly over his face.

Within seconds, massive amounts of electricity jolted his body. Three doses in all. Smoke curled up from the burning flesh. His fingers gripping the armrest curled back in convulsion. He was dead.

Doug Magee in *Slow Coming Dark*, a book against capital punishment

G

I would like Governor Graham to come and see me. If he had investigated my case he wouldn't be doing this. I know who I am. I want him to know whom he is killing – the real person, not some idea he has in his head about me.

John Spenkelink, speaking hours before his execution for first degree murder. (A US Governor signs death warrants and has the power to pardon criminals.)

Issues of life and death – Review task

A

B

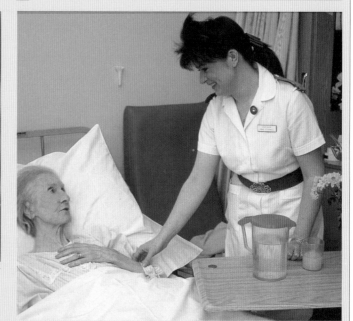

C

John Paul Harry, a prisoner on Death Row in Huntsville, Texas, USA

1 What name would be given to the deliberate taking of the life in each of the pictures on this page?

2 Choose two of the pictures and, for each, explain a possible viewpoint of a Christian who:
a) bases his/her response on absolutist principles;
b) bases his/her response on relativist principles.

3 Use at least two Bible passages to explain what Christians mean by the phrase 'sanctity of life' and why it is an important religious principle.

4 'No life is totally sacred.' Do you agree? Give reasons.

UNIT 3

Relationships

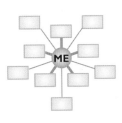

Your relationships connect you to other people.

Draw a large version of the diagram on the left at the centre of a sheet of paper, then add to it to show your own relationships. Show the strongest or most important connections with thick lines, the less important ones with thinner or dotted lines.

This is your relationships web!

In this unit you will investigate Christian attitudes to relationships.

3.1 The perfect relationship?

ACTIVITY

Either:

1   Choose one of the photos in **Source A** and complete a story web like this for your chosen photo:

   a) What is happening in the photo?

   b) What might have led to this moment?

   c) How might this relationship be sorted out?

Or:

2   Look back at the previous page and at your relationships web.

   a) Which of your relationships do you regard as 'good' ones? Which do you regard as 'bad'? Mark them with suitable symbols, for example ticks and crosses.

   b) At the moment, which do you think is your best relationship? Which do you think is your worst? Do you think these could change? How?

   c) Do you have any perfect relationships? If not, do you think there is such a thing as a perfect relationship?

   d) Do you ever feel lonely, despite all your relationships?

3   Working with a partner, draw up a list of qualities that you think characterise a good relationship.

A

3.2   Are Christian ideas about marriage out of date?

Popular attitudes to sex, marriage and divorce are changing in Britain. Today:

- Seventy per cent of couples live together before marriage
- Forty-one per cent of marriages end in divorce – an all-time high
- Britain has the highest divorce rate in Europe
- less than half the weddings in Britain take place in a church.

Despite these statistics, it is still the aim of the overwhelming majority of people in Britain to get married. And in a 1994 survey, 84 per cent of all women and 79 per cent of all men thought adultery was wrong.

Find out where you stand on the attitude scale with our Quick Quiz.

Are you the marrying kind?

1. Could you survive happily without a steady boyfriend or girlfriend for a few months?
   a) No! I'll go out with anyone to avoid being single.
   b) Yes! I don't want to rush into any old relationship.
   c) Definitely! I'm waiting for the perfect partner.
   d) Yes! I prefer being free.

2. How would you feel if, in the future, your parents tried to influence your choice of marriage partner?
   a) I'd be very cross! It's none of their business whom I marry.
   b) I wouldn't like to be pushed into something, but I would not rule out doing what they want.
   c) I'd be horrified. What a thought!
   d) I'd welcome their support. They know best.

3. Do you think it's OK to have sex before marriage?
   a) Yes! It builds up a relationship.
   b) No! I'd like to be a virgin when I get married.
   c) Definitely! I'm not going to get sex any other way.
   d) Maybe, but only if I intended to marry the person anyway.

4. Would you like to spend the whole of your life married to the same person?
   a) I can't imagine that at all. Boring!
   b) Nice idea, if it works.
   c) Of course! That's the whole point of marriage.
   d) I'd like it! If I manage to choose the right person in the first place.

5. Do you think that children are better off if their parents are married?
   a) Yes, absolutely! You shouldn't have children without marriage.
   b) It's more important for parents to be loving than to be married.
   c) Yes! I feel a happy marriage provides the best environment for children.
   d) No! Why should they be?

6. If you got married, would you have a religious ceremony?
   a) Definitely! I want a big white wedding in a church.
   b) I'd like a religious ceremony, but I can do without all the extras like presents and banquets.
   c) Some kind of ceremony, but not a religious one!
   d) I don't want any sort of wedding, religious or otherwise.

ARE YOU THE MARRYING KIND?

7. If you were married, how do you think you would react if your partner had an affair with someone else?
   a) I'd cope! These things happen, don't they?
   b) I'd be upset, but I'd work hard to rebuild the relationship.
   c) Shattered! I'd want a divorce immediately.
   d) I'd probably go off and do the same myself.

8. If you get married who will be the boss in your relationship?
   a) Husband in charge; wife to obey.
   b) Me! I love getting my own way.
   c) We'd be equals – you don't need anyone 'in charge' of a relationship.
   d) But I told you – I don't want to get married!

9. Your boyfriend/girlfriend suggests you get married. You are in love but you aren't sure you want to spend your lives together. What do you do?
   a) I'd say yes! We can always get divorced if it doesn't work out.
   b) I'd say no! I've got to be 100% certain. Divorce would be a disaster.
   c) I'd say maybe! Then talk over my fears with my partner.
   d) I don't want to get married.

ACTIVITY

1 On your own, try this quiz. Choose the answers that are closest to your own views. Be honest. Note down your answers on a separate sheet of paper.
2 When you have finished, work out with your teacher where you are on the attitude scale.
3 Compare your results with those of the rest of the class. Do you think your class is typical?
4 'Stop worrying about the relationship you haven't got, and start worrying about the relationships you have got!'
   Is this good advice? Do you think people today are too concerned about finding the right partner?

Key questions for Christians

- What is sex for?
- What is the point of marriage?
- What if marriage goes wrong?

What is sex for?

The Bible offers two distinct messages about sex.

Sex is to be celebrated …

According to the Bible, God's very first instruction to Adam and Eve was to go and have sex. The Bible says that when Creation was finished God thought everything – including sex – was very good! Sex is a pleasure, a gift and a joy. One of the most under-used books of the Bible is King Solomon's poem celebrating love and sex, *The Song of Songs,* also called *The Song of Solomon* (see Source A).

A

THE SONG OF SONGS

His eyes, too, are doves
      dipping in clear water
yet as if they had splashed in milk.
His cheeks are smooth couches
      scenting of spices.
His lips are red anemone-colour
moist with the breath of myrrh.
His arms are subtle as gold
      round
and studded with great jewels of Tarshish.
His rod is arrogant ivory
      flushed with sapphire-blue;
and his thighs are marble columns
      in sockets of pure gold.
Erect
   he looks like Lebanon
      a king among cedars.
But when he speaks it is soft and sweet.

  I love him
     whole and entire I love him.
This is my Beloved,
      women of Jerusalem,
Oh women.

Engraving and extract from a poetic adaptation of *The Song of Solomon,* published by the Ark Press

But sex is also to be controlled

Christianity teaches that sex belongs within marriage. Chastity (abstaining from sex before marriage) and fidelity (not having sex with anyone else once you are married) are valued very highly. 'Do not commit adultery' is one of the Ten Commandments. A common theme in the writing of St Paul in the New Testament is that Christians should not follow the sexual morality of the society around them but should aim for sexual restraint and control. For example, in writing to the Christians in the Greek city of Corinth – where promiscuity and prostitution were common – he said:

B

You know that your bodies are parts of the body of Christ. Shall I take a part of Christ's body and make it part of the body of a prostitute? Impossible! …

 Avoid immorality. Any other sin a man commits does not affect his body; but the man who is guilty of sexual immorality sins against his own body. Don't you know that your body is the temple of the Holy Spirit, who lives in you?

I Corinthians 6.15–19

C

True Love Waits

> ### *True Love Waits*
> Believing that true love waits, I make a commitment to God, myself, my family, those I date, my future mate and my future children to be sexually pure until the day I enter a covenant marriage relationship.
>
> **Jim Christensen**

A pledge card held by a 15-year-old member of the 'True Love Waits' movement, which began in Nashville, USA, in 1992. In a special ceremony, Christian children make a promise not to have sex before marriage. Parents give a ring to the child, saying 'let this ring be a constant reminder to you to be sexually pure.'

1　Compare Sources A and B. Both are from the Bible. Is there any contradiction between them? Explain your answer.
2　Read Source C. Do you think it is right for Christian parents to influence their children in their sexual lives? If so, at what age do you think it would be appropriate to use this ceremony?

Why do many Christians keep sex for marriage?

The negative 'control' message has been sounded rather more loudly by Christians in the past than the positive 'joy of sex' message. Sometimes this was for the purely practical reason that chastity has always been the surest method of contraception – for many centuries it was the only reliable method. However, many Christians would say that there are positive rather than negative reasons to keep sex for marriage (see Source D).

D

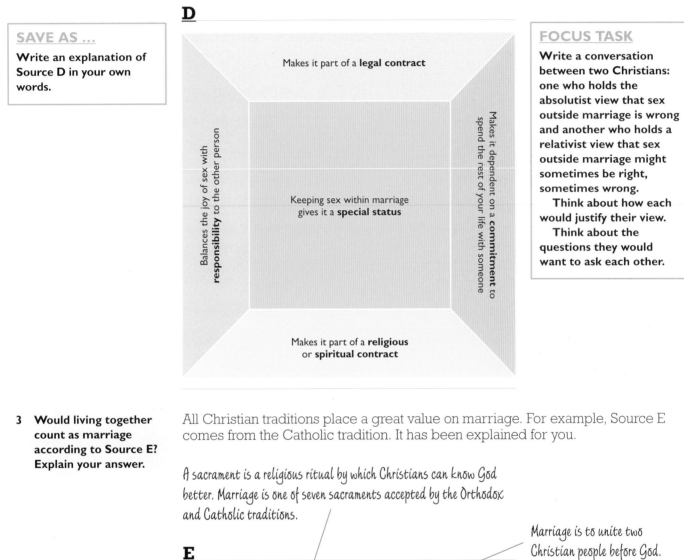

Makes it part of a **legal contract**

Balances the joy of sex with **responsibility** to the other person

Makes it dependent on a **commitment** to spend the rest of your life with someone

Keeping sex within marriage gives it a **special status**

Makes it part of a **religious** or **spiritual contract**

SAVE AS …

Write an explanation of Source D in your own words.

FOCUS TASK

Write a conversation between two Christians: one who holds the absolutist view that sex outside marriage is wrong and another who holds a relativist view that sex outside marriage might sometimes be right, sometimes wrong.

Think about how each would justify their view.

Think about the questions they would want to ask each other.

3 **Would living together count as marriage according to Source E? Explain your answer.**

All Christian traditions place a great value on marriage. For example, Source E comes from the Catholic tradition. It has been explained for you.

A sacrament is a religious ritual by which Christians can know God better. Marriage is one of seven sacraments accepted by the Orthodox and Catholic traditions.

Marriage is to unite two Christian people before God.

E

Marriage is the sacrament in which a baptised man and woman vow to belong to each other in a permanent, exclusive, sexual partnership of loving, mutual care, concern and shared responsibility in the hope of having children and bringing up a family.

From a catechism published by The Catholic Truth Society, 1985

Marriage is for life.

People should have only one wife or husband. This is known as monogamy.
    Sex outside marriage (adultery) is not permitted. 'Do not commit adultery' is the seventh of the Ten Commandments.

The couple are expected to have children.

Love and sex are important parts of the partnership.

Wife and husband help and support one another. The marriage relationship is as much about giving as taking.

What is a Christian marriage?

Wedding customs vary greatly from culture to culture. But there are some common elements across cultures:

- a public declaration – society is somehow involved and the ceremony requires a witness
- a marking of the forming of a new family unit
- vows made by the partners to commit themselves to one another for life.

Christian marriage usually begins with a church wedding. Each tradition has its own ceremonies, but Source F shows some common features.

1. A church wedding has many different elements. Discuss with a partner what is happening in the photographs in **Source G**.
2. Many people who do not attend church want to get married in church. Why do you think this is?
3. Should a minister or priest be prepared to marry non-churchgoers in a church? Give your reasons.

F

Order of Service

1 Hymn — *to focus everyone's minds on God*
2 Opening statement — *summarises what marriage is for (see Source I opposite)*
3 Declaration — *the witnesses and the couple are asked if there is any reason the couple cannot get married*
4 Promises or vows — *the couple make their promises to God and to one another in the presence of witnesses (see Source J)*
5 Exchange of rings
6 Proclamation — *the couple are now husband and wife*
7 Prayers for the couple — *and often a talk or a sermon about marriage*
8 The register is signed by the couple and witnesses — *to record that the marriage is legal*
9 Closing worship — *followed by photos and a reception or party*

SAVE AS ...

1 Each part of the marriage service is included for a reason. Some are legal, some are social and some are religious. Choose what you think are the four most important features from **Source F**. Explain why they are included and whether their purpose is legal, social or religious.
2 'Those whom God has joined, let no man separate.' These words of Jesus from Matthew 19.6 are often said in Anglican marriage services at the point when the couple are proclaimed husband and wife. Write a paragraph explaining whether you think it is an appropriate thing to say at a marriage service today.

G

1

2

Weddings in an Orthodox church in Bulgaria and a Protestant church in Hong Kong

H

1

It was the most wonderful day of my life ... so far. I passed from one stage of my life to another. It was like my baptism. There was the old me left behind on the other side of a gate. When I made my promises the new me, or the new us, took over on the other side. I felt different.

2

I went into it reluctantly - more for my family's sake than my own. We'd lived together for some years. We'd committed ourselves to each other long ago. But it did put a kind of seal on our relationship. A stamp of approval.

4 **How do the speakers in Source H differ in their attitude towards church weddings?**

5 **What do you think is the value to a Christian of getting married in a church?**

Promises, promises!

Because marriage is a major, life-long commitment, Churches prepare couples carefully for it. Marriage courses are common. Church leaders will counsel and pray with couples and discuss Christian teaching about marriage.

A wedding is a beginning, not an end. It should set you off in the right direction for a marriage journey. The real point is what follows. Let's look at the words that are said and the promises that are made at the marriage service.

I

... marriage is a gift of God in creation ... a holy mystery in which man and woman become one flesh. It is God's purpose that husband and wife shall be united in love as Christ is united with his Church.

Marriage is given,

that a husband and wife may comfort and help each other, living faithfully together in need and in plenty, in sorrow and in joy ...

that with delight and tenderness they may know each other in love, and, through the joy of their bodily union, may strengthen the union of their hearts and lives ...

that they may have children and be blessed in caring for them and bringing them up in accordance with God's will, to his praise and glory.

In marriage husband and wife belong to one another, and they begin a new life together in the community. It is a way of life that all should honour; and it must not be undertaken carelessly, lightly or selfishly, but reverently, responsibly, and after serious thought ...

we pray with them, that, strengthened and guided by God, they may fulfil his purpose for the whole of their earthly life together.

Abridged from the Anglican marriage service in *The Alternative Service Book*, 1980

J

I take you to be my
husband/wife,
To have and to hold
From this day forward,
For better, for worse,
For richer, for poorer,
In sickness and in health,
To love and to cherish
Till death us do part,
According to God's
holy law.
And to this I pledge myself.

A vow like this is used in most Christian marriage services.

ACTIVITY

1 **Read Sources I and J. Draw up two lists:**
   a) **what is expected of the married couple;**
   b) **qualities that the couple will need.**
2 **Elaine Storkey, an evangelical writer, has said, 'Despite expensive weddings, every marriage in the West gets off to a bad start because we have to unlearn individualism and learn community.' What do you think she means? Do you agree with her? Refer to Sources I and J in your answer.**

Married to God?

Not everyone wants to get married. Others want to, but never meet the right partner. A small number of Christians decide not to marry because they want to devote their life to God instead. Some traditions, such as the Catholic Church, reserve a high place for those such as priests, monks or nuns who take this vow of celibacy.

Family values

Having children and bringing up a family is a central purpose of Christian marriage (see Checkpoint on page 42).

Source K introduces you to one Christian family. The Wells are members of a growing independent evangelical Church which started seven years ago on a new housing development near Nottingham. The Church meets in a school, or uses homes, pubs or hired rooms for its various activities. It devises its own services and is not connected with any 'denomination'. All the family help in the Church: Paul is the minister, Jane leads children's activities, Becky and Chris, their children, sometimes provide music.

1   **Read Source K. Would you like to be part of the Wells family? Give reasons.**

2   **How can you tell from their family life that the Wells are a Christian family?**

K

Paul

The Christian family is a tool to shape us. In the Bible God says to the Israelites, 'What you have learned from me, you should pass on to your children and your children's children.' We try to pass on our values. But Jane and I also change and grow from the experience of family life. Family life exposes all your weaknesses. What you are in the family is what you are! It's a chilling thought that we pass on what we are! Bringing up a family is the greatest responsibility most parents will ever have.

I don't like legalism. It's all about attitudes and perspective – having a God-like attitude to money, or your work, or the rest of your family. We don't tell our children do this or do that, we try to encourage them to reflect Christian values in their relationships with others – forgiveness, trust, etc. Young children might need do's and don'ts, but teenagers need their own clear and firm set of values to guide them in the decisions they have to make.

We do a lot of things together. We try to keep Sunday special. We don't do any big shopping on Sundays – just emergencies. Sunday should not be just like any other day. In fact, at a service last week I suggested a minute's mourning silence for Nat West Bank because they had just opened the first Sunday bank.

Jane

I love children. I am sometimes tempted to hold on to them too tightly. I have to learn that they are God's and have to be handed back.

My family has always come first for me, but as they have got older I have been home-tutoring children excluded from school and I have also been fostering for the local authority. We had one family of three under-fives for 16 months, so you can imagine that this has to be a whole family commitment. Everyone has to support it. We prayed about it and agreed it together. Becky and Chris are brilliant with small children.

In difficult situations we try to listen to one another and see each other's point of view; we think about how Jesus would react in this situation. Using the Bible to make decisions is not about looking for a text in the Bible, but about thinking your way into what attitude Jesus would take.

Going to Church together is very important. We've always done this. The children have always been involved. It's something we all share. But I think we still don't spend enough time together as a family. I don't think we discuss small decisions together enough.

The Wells family

Becky

Time together

Families need to spend time together. This is a priority for the Wells. They all say that it is a shame that Paul's job forces him to spend many evenings working. Even so, Becky and Chris estimate that they spend about six or seven hours a week talking about significant things with either of their parents. This compares with a recent survey which found that, on average, teenagers in Christian families spend just 23 minutes a week talking to their fathers and 38 minutes a week talking to their mothers.

I'm just starting A levels. Ever since I was a young child I have read the Bible with my parents. Until three years ago we prayed together every day. We don't now. Partly that's because we got slack when we fostered three under-fives, but also it was part of Chris and I growing up and working out our own relationships with God. I pray on my own. Life is 100 times easier if you pray about things. But I had to get my own faith, not rely on my parents'.

Neither of us were baptised as children. Mum and Dad had a thanksgiving and dedication service when I was a few months old, but baptism is for when you decide for yourself. I'm going to be baptised next Easter.

We spend time together – not enough because Dad's job takes him out many evenings, but we have good quality time together. We spend better time together as a family than any of my friends' families seem to manage.

3 Paul Wells says, 'It's not the amount of time a family spends together that matters, it's the kind of time.'
   a) **What do you think he means?**
   b) **How far do you agree with him?**
4 Orthodox, Catholic and some Protestant Churches use infant baptism to welcome babies into the Church, followed by first communion or confirmation. Others – particularly Baptists – have an infant dedication, followed by 'believers baptism' in which people decide as adults whether to follow that religion. **What do you think are the advantages and disadvantages of each approach?**

FOCUS TASK

Here are some of the things the Wells listed as their family values:
*   forgiveness and acceptance
*   being ready to change
*   thinking of others before yourself
*   being honest with one another
*   finding God's will.

1 Choose two values from the list and find examples in the statements above of how this value affects the Wells' family life.
2 Draw or describe a pair of cartoons showing:
   a) family life without these values;
   b) family life with these values.

God doesn't pass or fail you. He cares whether you pass or fail but he accepts you as you are. In the family everyone should be accepted for who they are.

Our faith affects the way we spend our money. We have tried to buy what we need rather than what we want, although I still want a Chrysler Voyager. I actually think we need that too! But we can't afford it, so . . .

As a family, we never let problems get out of hand. When we have arguments we try to forgive and forget quickly. We always try to sort out bad feelings before bedtime. Just praying together or reading the Bible as a family doesn't mean anything on its own. It's actions that count –hypocrites say all the right things but then don't do what God wants. We spend good time together: going to watch Notts County, church, meals, walking the dog, playing snooker.

Chris

Pressures on family life

There are many pressures on Christian families today. Society is largely secular (non-religious). Practising Christians are in a small minority. Christian teenagers sometimes feel their family values are at odds with those of their peers. They may feel their family's values to be old-fashioned or limiting.

Some Christians argue that the importance of Sunday as a day of rest or as a religious festival has been eroded by Sunday trading and Sunday working, as well as by increased leisure opportunities at the weekend. Christian families have to struggle to keep Sunday special when the nation sees it as a day of leisure rather than as a religious festival. Even many Christian families have dropped some of the habits which once formed the backbone of Christian family life – grace before meals; praying and Bible reading together; going to church together (just a generation ago, twice on a Sunday was not unusual).

Some say that the traditional nuclear or extended family unit as the building block of society is under threat. Patterns of family life are changing. Debt and fear of unemployment have led to many breadwinners working longer or antisocial hours. Many more mothers have paid employment outside the home than 20 years ago. At the same time, the proportion of families with no employed members has increased.

The proportion of one-parent families has quadrupled in the last 30 years. People move around more. Children move away from parents and, as a result, there are more young people and old people who live alone.

Images of the family

L

Television is often blamed for damaging family life. Teenagers spend up to 20 hours per week watching – which leaves little time for family life. A more subtle criticism is that television programmes undermine family values. This is how the argument runs: on the one hand, there are the soap operas; the typical soap family has broken marriages, money worries, alcohol problems, even domestic violence. On the other hand, there is the sitcoms' or the advertisers' typical family with its perfect kitchen; smiling, long-suffering parents; cheerful, healthy children. Most families live between these two extremes, yet these images affect us. The perfect family makes us less willing to work on our own family relationships when things get tough. The awful soap family makes us accept destructive behaviour as normal.

ACTIVITY

Do your own survey of images of the family as seen on television. Work with a partner to analyse one evening's output of soap operas and advertisements. Think about which family values are emphasised and how these support or conflict with Christian family values. You can get a survey sheet from your teacher to help you to do your research and write up your findings.

FOCUS TASK

1   Write the word 'marriage' in the centre of a large sheet of paper.

2   As a class or in small groups, brainstorm the different problems that lead to marriages failing. Write these problems around the centre.

3   These problems are often symptoms of deeper problems. Leading off each problem, write the deeper factors which may underlie it.

4   List ways in which Christians might help people whose marriages are in difficulty.

5   Ideas about the best way to choose a marriage partner vary from culture to culture. What would a Christian say are the advantages and disadvantages of each of the following:

   a) choosing someone yourself because you fall in love with them

   b) your parents choosing someone for you?

1   How might a Christian react to Source M?

✓ CHECKPOINT

Some traditions see marriage as a SACRAMENT – something made by God which cannot be dissolved. Others see it as a contract or COVENANT. A contract is an agreement between two people to do (or not to do) something.

A covenant means the same – but usually carries with it the idea that the contract is drawn up in the sight of God.

When marriages fail

Throughout the history of the Christian Church its leaders have had to recognise that Christians fall short of God's standards for marriage. Many marriages run into problems. What then?

Marriage guidance

Many Christians are deeply involved in marriage guidance counselling. They talk with couples whose relationships have problems and try to resolve them.

Many ministers, priests and Christian counsellors find that a large amount of time is spent helping people sort out marriage problems.

Divorce

Divorce is forbidden by some Christian traditions. The Catholic Church, for example, teaches that marriage is a 'sacrament', i.e. something made by God. No human agent has the right or the power to unmake something made by God. A divorce decree is therefore as meaningless as saying 'I was never born'; the couple were joined by God and nothing can unjoin them except death, although in extreme cases a marriage can be annulled. Churches that do not allow divorce train priests and counsellors to support couples whose marriages are failing.

Some Christian traditions do allow divorce. They see marriage as a contract or a covenant (see Checkpoint). It ought not to be broken but it can be, and provision must be made for this. Jesus said that divorce was allowed, but only because the hardness of people's hearts made it inevitable that some marriages would not work.

Remarriage?

Some Churches allow divorcees to remarry in church, others do not. The Church of Scotland, for instance, remarries divorced people if the minister is convinced of their sincere commitment to the new relationship. Remarriage is seen as a sign of God's forgiveness and willingness to give people a new start.

M

O-kay! Can we have the bride's mother and stepfather with respective offspring by various couplings, the bride's father and his live-in-lover with their new baby, the groom's father and his partner Bob, his mother who took it badly at first but is over the worst, the chief bridesmaid who was engaged to the groom until so recently and her therapist, without whom she wouldn't be here today – good! Everybody happy?

1 The law no longer requires one party to be at fault in a divorce. Is it helpful to use words like 'fault' when discussing marital breakdown?

2 Read Source O. Why do you think some clergy want such a service?

3 Why do you think it has not been accepted by the Bishops?

4 What are the arguments for and against such services being made available in Christian Churches?

5 If society's attitudes change, should the attitudes of the Church change to fit in? Explain your answer.

Divorce recovery

Some Churches have arranged divorce recovery workshops, where divorced Church members can talk through their experiences, learn from others who have been through similar experiences and be helped to build new lives.

Some Anglican priests have devised their own 'divorce services' to recognise the breakdown of a marriage, to mark its ending and release people from vows they are unable to fulfil. Revd Margaret Blackall drew on her own experience of divorce in writing the service she uses (see Source O). The Anglican synod was asked to approve such services for official Church use but has so far refused.

N

[After my divorce] one of the most difficult things to deal with was that I had stood up, in front of the people whom I loved the most, and before God, and made solemn promises, which I meant at the time, but which later I was unable to keep when I realised that this was not the right relationship for me. I felt very stupid and guilty and felt like a failure. I had let people down. I felt like a bad person. It takes a long time to get over these things.

I left the Church for a long time because I felt so guilty and out of place. I thought everyone was looking at me and seeing a bad person. I removed myself before they could get at me!

Now I am back at Church because the Church I go to is full of people who accept me for myself. They don't ask nosy questions about my past and they do not judge me for it.

A young woman, divorced after just two and a half years of marriage, explains her feelings about the divorce three years later.

ACTIVITY

Source O gives only a rough outline of what might feature in a divorce service. Plan your own detailed ceremony. Include:
• an opening explanation
• vows
• actions
• appropriate music, dress, setting, etc.

Would people who believe that marriage is a sacrament be happy to use your service?

O

The service has confession, commitment and healing. There is also thanksgiving for what was good in the marriage, including the birth of children. When you come to a funeral, you are burying a body.
A divorced person needs that experience of a funeral and the opportunity to say a goodbye.

Revd Margaret Blackall

P

[These services] make me extremely sad. There is an urgent need for the Church to get its act together at a time when the institution of marriage needs underpinning.

Charles Colchester of the evangelical campaigning group CARE

FOCUS TASK

1 Do you think that Christians largely agree or disagree about marriage?
Explain your answer.

2 Look back to your answers to the quiz on page 35. Have any of your views changed as a result of studying Christian ideas about marriage and divorce?

3 Source E on page 37 comes from a catechism. This is a method of teaching Christian ideas. Write a modern catechism explaining different aspects of Christian teaching about marriage. Each sentence should start:

• Sex is …
• Marriage is …
• Divorce is …

3.3 Why do Christians disagree about homosexuality?

A

✓ **CHECKPOINT**

The Lesbian and Gay Christian Movement

Forty years ago in Britain you would have found a strong consensus among Christians that homosexuality was wrong. Gay Christians either denied their sexuality or kept it secret. At that time the Christian attitude was backed by law, which forbade homosexual sex between men although not between women.

In 1967 the law was changed to permit homosexual acts between consenting adult men. In the 1970s the gay liberation movements encouraged many 'closet' homosexuals to declare that they were gay.

At this time the Lesbian and Gay Christian Movement (LGCM) was started, in order to encourage a more sympathetic attitude towards homosexuality within the Church and to support gay Christians who 'came out' after years of hiding their sexuality.

The service in Southwark Cathedral in 1996 was a celebration of the 20th anniversary of the founding of the LGCM.

Welcome for gays

THE BISHOP of Guildford held out the vision of an 'inclusive Church' to the Lesbian and Gay Christian Movement (LGCM) in Southwark Cathedral last Saturday, when he preached at the movement's 20th-anniversary service.

But he also warned that there was still a conflict between its and the Church's understandings of the Christian tradition. 'We cannot solve our dilemma by turning cohabitation or same-sex relationships into marriage.'

The congregation applauded his sermon at length; and afterwards he told reporters that he was 'amazed' by the response. 'I thought they were much more generous to me than the sermon deserved.'

The LGCM's general secretary, the Revd Richard Kirker, said that LGCM members would welcome the call for inclusivity, but there remained 'clear water' between their view and that of the House of Bishops.

More than 2000 people queued in the dark to be present in the cathedral or to watch the service on screens in the Glaziers Hall nearby. They were barracked by demonstrators. Banners proclaimed: 'Sodomy, lesbianism, a perversion to be repented of, not an orientation to be celebrated'.

But inside the cathedral, the mood was genial and sometimes openly affectionate.

Milk sweetened with honey was distributed in connection with a reading from Exodus, and a hymn was sung: 'The love that dares to question, The love that speaks its name'.

Reform, the Evangelical group which is attacking the service as a 'festival of gay sex', held about 40 counter-events across the country; and one of the organisers said later that about 200 people, including the Bishops of Southwark and Kingston, had taken part in the 12-hour prayer vigil organised not far down-river in St Mary Magdalen's, Bermondsey.

Glyn Paflin,
in the *Church Times*,
22 November 1996

ACTIVITY

Read Source A.

1 What was the service celebrating?
2 What were the protesters objecting to?
3 Where would you prefer to have been: in the church celebrating or outside the church protesting? Explain why.
4 The Bishop of Southwark went to both the LGCM service and the prayer vigil organised by the protest group Reform. Why do you think he did this?
5 Why do you think this service was so controversial?

Key questions for Christians

- Is homosexuality God-given?
- How can the Church show love towards homosexuals?
- How can gay people play a full role in the Church?

Different Christian views on homosexuality

There is very little consensus in the Church on the issue of homosexuality; it divides Christians at a basic level. There are practising homosexuals in the Church – some in positions of leadership. There are also many people who are opposed to homosexuality, some of them bitterly. Some gays and lesbians feel accepted by the Church; others feel rejected and excluded.

Within any one denomination you might find all the views represented below. This produces a confusing picture.

Homosexuality is absolutely wrong	Homosexual tendencies are natural and acceptable; homosexual sex is not	Homosexual relationships are sometimes acceptable. They should be judged by the same standards as all human relationships	Homosexual sex is a wonderful God-given gift to be celebrated
If you are gay or lesbian it cannot be the will of God. You need to change. If you do not repent, the consequences might be dire for you or for others.	If you are gay or lesbian it is not your fault; you did not choose to be that way. Do not deny those feelings. Enjoy friendships with others of the same sex. However, do not have homosexual sex. That would be against the will of God.	Homosexuality is a natural part of some people. So homosexual sex is acceptable as long as it is expressed within the ideal Christian relationship – i.e. within a faithful, monogamous relationship where both partners consent.	God made human beings with their sexuality. God loves and accepts us as we are. Sexuality is not an added extra that can be separated from a person. It is basic, and expressing it is essential and good.

ACTIVITY

1 Read Sources B–J and explain where you would place each speaker on the above scale.
2 Where would you put yourself on the scale? Explain your position.

B

Why write and circulate a booklet on homosexual practice? Am I implying that it is more serious than other sins? Or is it evidence of a hang-up about sexuality?

No, this sin is only one of many which bedevil the Church. But homosexual practice has come to have major strategic importance as a serious sin which the Church of England and other denominations are in danger of officially tolerating and which some Christians justify.

Were the Church to tolerate officially or even bless such practice it would experience division and other damage. It could lead to the break-up of the Anglican Communion. And if the Church were to justify any sin officially, including this one, we would incur divine judgement. This could take the form of further, even massive, decline in numbers and influence. We would also contribute to the moral confusion in the nation which undermines the fabric of society.

Evangelical priest Tony Higton in the preface to his booklet *What does the Bible say about homosexual practice?* which was distributed to all Anglican clergy before the 1997 Synod debate on homosexuality

FOCUS TASK

Source B was written in preparation for a Church debate on homosexuality. Imagine you are a news reporter making a radio programme about this debate. You have to interview some of the delegates who will be speaking at the debate. You want to make sure your programme reflects the wide range of opinions within the Church.

Work in a small group to devise a short radio feature with interviews and links expressing the range of viewpoints on this issue. Sources A–J will give you some ideas.

C

Love is accepting all aspects of our nature, including our creativity, our intellect, our various faults and abilities, our colour, our sex and our sexuality. When we learn how to love, we learn also how to worship.

Quaker report

D

You can't have different rules for different people. The overall message of Jesus is love and that is all we are doing.

Anonymous Gay Christian

E

... there should be an open and welcoming place in the Christian community ... for those who are conscientiously convinced that a faithful, sexually active [homosexual] relationship with one other person, aimed at helping both partners to grow in discipleship, is the way of life God wills for them.

From a 1991 Church of England report giving the Bishops' views on homosexuality

F

A poster carried by an anti-gay protester at a rally in South Africa. The poster was used in a pre-general election advertisement in the magazine *The Big Issue* in 1997. AIDS has particularly affected the gay community. Some hard line anti-gays have interpreted AIDS as God's punishment for sexual immorality.

G

To love another, whether of the same sex or of a different sex, is to have entered the area of the richest human experience, but that experience of love is spoiled when we do not think or act as God wills us to think or act.

Catholic Archbishop Basil Hume. The Catholic Church teaches that homosexual sex is a sin.

H

Whilst we are not responsible for what we are, we are accountable for what we do; and homosexual conduct like heterosexual conduct is controllable.

Statement from the Salvation Army

I

A lapel badge distributed by the LGCM

J

I believed I was going to Hell. Dealing with this was harder than being called names or being rejected by my peers. For five years I continued going to Church but I was only going through the motions. I still believed in God, but I had no real feeling that God believed in me.

Then, when I was 20, my best friend introduced me to a wise and wonderful pastor who opened my eyes and helped me to re-open my heart. Together, he and I read the Bible passages that had plagued my life. He interpreted the Bible in a very different way from the way I had been brought up to understand it.

He said I had been given life by God, and being gay was a part of the whole Me that God had created. I was still the same person I had always been. I began to realise that God loved me as much now as he did when I was ten years old. It was such a relief to know that I could be a Christian who was gay.

James, a practising Christian who is also gay.

DISCUSS

1 **How might each of these principles, which Christians apply to heterosexual relationships, be applied to a homosexual relationship:**
   • **commitment**
   • **responsibility**
   • **chastity**
   • **fidelity?**
2 **Look back at the church service referred to in Source A on page 45. Imagine that James (Source J) was asked to give 'the welcome' at that service. What might he have said?**

Read Source K and the two interpretations of it.
Then write your answers to these questions.

1 How do the commentators differ in their views on homosexuality?

2 How do they differ in their views on the Bible?

3 Which of these words might apply to each view: evangelical, literalist, liberal, absolutist, tolerant, modern? Explain your choice with reference to the points they make.

4 In your own words, explain why it is possible for Christians to interpret the Bible in different ways.

5 Which attitude to the Bible do you find more convincing? Why?

How can the Bible guide Christian attitudes to homosexuality?

Homosexuality is not mentioned in the gospels. Elsewhere, the Bible condemns homosexuality, but such passages are interpreted very differently by opponents and supporters of gay rights.

Source K is one such passage. The notes show two different interpretations of it. Many evangelicals take the view on the left. They tend to take the Bible literally and maintain quite a hard line against homosexuality. Liberals are more likely to take the view on the right. They are aware of the Bible's anti-homosexuality passages but see them as an unhelpful guide on this issue. They point to other biblical principles as being more important in the present day, taking the view that, in certain situations, homosexual relationships may be accepted by God.

You must read this in the context of the whole Bible. Without exception, wherever the Bible refers to homosexuality, it condemns it. For example in the Old Testament it says, 'No man is to have sexual relations with another man; God hates that.' (Leviticus 18.22). Leviticus 20.13 adds that the punishment for homosexual acts is that offenders 'shall be put to death'. There are many other examples throughout the Old Testament and the New Testament. This passage is just one example.

The core argument against homosexuality in this passage is that female and male homosexuality are both contrary to God's created order. Sex between men and women is part of God's plan. Homosexuality is not.

Paul was not writing only for his own time. He was inspired by God to write things that apply to all Christians for all time. Messages of the Bible such as this are as relevant today as they ever have been. We undermine the authority of the whole Bible if we accept one bit and ignore others.

K

Even the women pervert the natural use of their sex by unnatural acts. In the same way the men give up natural sexual relations with women and burn with passion for each other. Men do shameful things with each other, and as a result they bring upon themselves the punishment they deserve for their wrongdoing.

Romans 1.26–27

You must read this in its own context. This is one verse from a long passage about what happens when people worship 'idols'. It is not actually about homosexuality, but about idol worship. What Paul (the writer) is really condemning is idol worship and what it leads to. We should not read this as a clear condemnation of all homosexual practices. Most of the other passages in the Bible which condemn homosexuality are really condemning other things associated with it.

Homosexuality is in some people's nature – it is natural for them. What Paul is condemning is those who indulge in unnatural homosexual sex – presumably those who do it just for fun. The homosexuality which Paul is referring to would have been exploitative, probably without the consent of both parties. You can't generalise about all homosexuality from this. Paul may not have been aware of homosexuality between two loving, consenting individuals.

Paul was working in a different cultural context. Many of his values would be questioned today. For example, he accepts slavery; no Christian would do so today. In the same way, his attitude to homosexuality may not be relevant today. We have to reinterpret the Bible in the light of today's culture.

We should look elsewhere in the Bible for our guide to how God views homosexuality today – to the principles of love and compassion, to God's offer of fullness of life to all.

3.4 How do Christians respond to racism?

A

Case study: The Ogunwobi family

Sunday Ogunwobi arrived in Britain from Nigeria in 1981. He came as a student. His wife Bunmi came soon after. Their first child was born in 1987, their second in 1989. Bunmi worked to support the family. Sunday continued as a student. He was also an elder of his Church, and a governor of his children's school.

However, in 1994 the Home Office decided Sunday had been in Britain too long and refused an extension of his visa. A deportation order was served to send him back to Nigeria. He appealed. In March 1994 Bunmi had their third child. The first two children were both needing sustained medical treatment. Sunday had been offered a job with a local project helping unemployed young people to find jobs.

On the eve of his deportation Sunday decided, with the support of local Church leaders, to go into sanctuary as a last resort. His wife was then observed (she said harassed) by immigration officials. Two weeks later she and the children joined him in the church. After ten months they met immigration officials but the deportation order was not lifted. They were visited by the American Civil Rights leader Jesse Jackson, who promised to take up their case with the United Nations.

In 1997, after more than three years in sanctuary, they were given permission to stay in Britain, and moved into their own home.

Adapted from *Race for the Millennium* by David Haslam of the Churches' Commission for Racial Justice

David Haslam would argue that the Ogunwobi family were victims of 'institutionalised racism', i.e. racist attitudes that are part of the way institutions in this country are set up. For example, white people are less likely to be deported.

Such views have angered other Christian people, however. They argue that the Ogunwobi case was not about race, but about the principle of whether the government has a right to control immigration. They say that as long as the government applies the law equally and fairly to all people it is not at fault.

ACTIVITY

1 **Copy the chart below onto paper and use Source A to help you to complete it.**

Reasons why the Ogunwobi family should have been allowed to stay	Reasons why the Home Office would want them to leave

2 **Do you think that the Church was right to offer sanctuary to the Ogunwobi family?**
3 **Do you think the government's treatment of the Ogunwobi family could be described as racist? Make sure you give reasons for your views.**

Key questions for Christians

- Is the Church racist?
- How can Christians help repair the damage done by racism?

B

Racism has no part in the Christian Gospel. It contradicts our Lord's command to love our neighbours as ourselves. It offends the fundamental Christian belief that every person is made in the image of God and is equally precious. It solves no problems and creates nothing but hatred and fear.'

George Carey, Archbishop of Canterbury

C

This 'Divider' God is sinister and evil: a god who is historically on the side of the White settlers, who dispossesses Black people of their land and who gives the major part of the land to his 'chosen people'. The god of the South African State is not merely a false god, it is the devil disguised as Almighty God – the antichrist.

From *The Kairos Document*, 1985

ACTIVITY A

Imagine you are a member of a Church in Britain during the 1980s. Use the information above to write a letter to the DRC explaining why you, as a Christian, are ashamed of their official beliefs. You might like to encourage them to read *The Kairos Document*, although you will need to explain why.

*W*hat do Christians believe about racism?

Most Christians would argue that all people are created in God's image and that all people are created equal. They might look to the Bible and find passages like Paul's Letter to the Galatians, which states, 'There is no difference between Jews and Gentiles, between slaves and free people, between men and women; you are all one in union with Christ Jesus' (Galatians 3.28). This attitude is supported by statements from Church leaders (see Source B, for example).

Although there are many Christians all over the world fighting racism, there are also examples of racism in the Christian Church. One of the most extreme examples has been in the Dutch Reformed Church of South Africa (DRC).

<u>S</u>outh Africa: racist theology

The white-dominated DRC argued that God had deliberately divided the people of the world into different races and that white people were made to be superior to black people. The DRC argued that passages such as Galations 3.28 (see above) mean that people are spiritually equal, not physically equal.

The DRC believed that the racist apartheid laws in South Africa were God's will. It argued that races should be kept separate, that white people should have better opportunities than black people, that mixed marriages and relationships should not be encouraged so that the different races stayed 'pure'.

The DRC used the Bible to support its views. It presented God as 'the Great Divider'. It said, for example, that the Creation story shows God dividing everything into separate categories (see Genesis 1). In the same way, white is divided from black and is meant to be kept separate. These racist beliefs were used to support the apartheid regime introduced in 1948.

<u>S</u>outh Africa: the anti-racist response

Other South-African Christians opposed the racist views of the DRC.

In 1982 the Dutch Reformed Mission Church (DRMC) declared a 'state of confession' as a protest against Christian apartheid beliefs. In 1985, 50 theologians based in and around Soweto, a black township, published their beliefs in *The Kairos Document* (Source C). This accused the DRC of 'misusing biblical texts for its own political purposes'. These developments helped to change the official views of the DRC. The DRC later publicly repented of their views.

Many anti-apartheid Christians in South Africa faced a bitter dilemma. They believed that the apartheid regime was wrong but it was supported by all the power of the South African state police and army. To fight apartheid was to be branded a Communist or a terrorist; you were liable to be imprisoned, tortured or murdered.

The question was whether to fight violence with violence or with non-violence. Some Christians joined the armed struggle against apartheid. Many more, including South African Church leader, Archbishop Desmond Tutu, chose non-violent methods, such as leading protest marches and collecting signatures for petitions. This is an issue that Christians in many countries have had to consider. You will return to it in detail on page 62.

D

Desmond Tutu arguing his case with a white apartheid supporter

Images of Jesus

The way we picture Jesus can be racist.

E

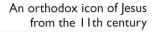

An orthodox icon of Jesus
from the 11th century

ACTIVITY B

Study Sources E–G.

1   Write down the messages about Jesus that you think each image portrays.
2   Which image comes closest to the way you picture Jesus?
3   Which image do you think comes closest to the real appearance of Jesus?
4   No one knows what Jesus actually looked like. Is this an advantage or a disadvantage to Christians who are fighting racism?
5   Read Source H. Compare this image of Jesus with Sources E–G. How is it different or similar?

G

The Baptism of Christ by a modern Haitian artist

F

Christ depicted in a painting by Edward A. Armitage (1869)

H

Messiah Man

I am getting weary from listening to deceit
From people in a hurry to change my society
I and I a victim of Babylon history
Political immorality has taken my memory

Wise man say the system never shall change
Jah man say until the people have changed
My people live in sorrow, no food for the children to eat
No hopes for a better tomorrow and this is to say the least

Messiah is watching over your activities
Soon he is returning to judge all your practices
Wise man say the system never shall change
Jah man say until the people have changed,
people have changed

I say we need Messiah Man

From *Messiah Man* by Ben Okafor

Challenging racism in British Churches

Racism in Britain seldom takes the extreme form that it did in apartheid South Africa. Nevertheless it exists, even if it is more hidden. A survey on racism in the Church of England in 1988 revealed:

- a lack of black leaders
- racism in Church schools
- a lack of participation by black Church members
- a lack of equal opportunities in employment in the Church of England
- a belief that racism is only an issue in inner-city areas where people from ethnic minority groups live.

I

When I first came to this country I went to the local church because that was the denomination I attended back home in Ghana.

A well-meaning lady came over to me and whispered kindly, 'This isn't your Church, dear. It's up the road!'

Refusing to listen to my explanations, she led me by the arm to the door and pointed to another building about 100 yards away.

It was a black-led Church.

Patrick, aged 60

J

A member of my mother's Church stood in the local council elections. He was well respected among other people and had been the Church's missionary secretary for some time. We were shocked to find that he was standing for the National Front (an openly racist political party).

Charles, aged 40

K

There's this young white lad who read both the Bible readings during the service last week. I've only seen him here once before and there he was out at the front reading the lessons. And people noticed. When he walked out the front, Jean looked at Mavis, Mavis looked at me and I looked at the floor. You know, hardly ever is a black person called out to do anything at the front. It's like they don't even think to ask if any of us would like to do anything. It's not that we always want to be at the front. Just that we'd like the opportunity to turn it down if we wanted to. It's obvious and so hurtful.

Michelle, in her 40s

L

Colour is good, Lord God,
Some people are saying that you are colour blind,
that you don't care whether a person is black or white,
or any other colour,
and so we shouldn't care either.

Well, I can't accept that.

People are important!
Their eyes are important, their names are important,
their race is important, and their colour is important.

A prayer written by a New Zealand Christian

DISCUSS

1 **Read Sources I–K. In what ways are people being racist in each one?**
2 **Which would you say is the most serious example of racism? Explain why.**
3 **How could Christians deal with each of the situations described?**
4 **How might the following passages in the Bible help a Christian person to react appropriately to any of these situations:**
   - **Matthew 6.14–15?**
   - **Mark 2.15–17?**
5 **Read Source L. How far do you think this is a helpful attitude to take in combatting racism in Britain?**

SAVE AS . . .

6 **Explain the difference between prejudice and discrimination, using examples from pages 49–52.**

<u>S</u>eparate or together?

For some black Christians in Britain the pain inflicted by racism in the mainstream denominations has been too great. They have formed their own 'black-led' Churches.

Others have chosen to remain within the main denominations. The Right Revd John Sentamu is the Bishop of Stepney. His appointment has been welcomed by many people, but particularly those wanting to see greater representation of minority ethnic groups in the power structures of the Church of England.

As a Bishop in East London he is well aware of the many issues that affect people from ethnic minority groups and he has tried to use his power and influence to help people wherever possible.

> Almost as soon as I began work here I tried to play my role in trying to sort out accommodation for the chaplain at the Royal London [Hospital], a Muslim whose housing was pretty poor. So I knocked on doors and kicked and screamed and he got a four-bedroomed house.
>
> Also ... the British Government was trying to deport a Muslim mother with a severely disabled British child ... so the child would have been left and the mother would have to go back to Nigeria ... I wrote letters to the Queen, to the Prime Minister and she's been allowed to stay. Because the Church of England is established, you've got access to certain areas ... it sometimes opens doors to things ... one is able to cut through red tape very fast.

Bishop Sentamu is Chairman of the Committee for Minority Ethnic Anglican Concerns. He believes that there are many signs of hope in the Church of England. Problems of racism are being openly addressed and strategies to help tackle racism in the future are being put into place.

This doesn't mean that the Church of England is in any way perfect. There is still a hard core of people in the Church who feel that, because there are no black people in their local church, they have no racism. This view is not supported by the General Synod of the Church of England, its decision-making body.

> The 1990 report, *Seeds of Hope*, identified that the structures, not the people, of the Church of England were very racist in the way that they operated. Because they were originally built on the basis that anything white is normal, they tend to have a bias against black people, so the Church of England set up a survey and a discussion of how the institution could stop being racist in its application.
>
> The title of the second report, *The Passing Winter*, was chosen because a lot of people had been frozen out of the Church of England, so had left it and gone to join black Churches. Because of the work that has been done over the past five years, we are able to make changes in the institution itself. So the winter is passing – but it still hasn't gone, which means there are still people with racist attitudes, racist views, racist ideas.
>
> The Church of England itself has taken very seriously the findings of these two reports and has been quite brave in admitting its racism ... It has been more honest than society at large about what is going on. Getting the Race Relations Act brought in was a major piece of work by the Churches ... The Church has been quite clear: everybody is made in God's image, of equal worth.

FOCUS TASK

Racism is not only morally unacceptable, it is also illegal in many cases. The British law makes it an offence to incite racial hatred or to discriminate on the grounds of race.

Every school has to have an equal opportunities policy to ensure that they are fighting racism in the classroom and in the school organisation. Maurice Hobbs of the group Evangelical Christians for Racial Justice argues that churches should also have equal opportunities policies.

Working in groups, create a statement summarising Christian attitudes to racism which could be included in a local church's anti-racism policy. It should set out:

- **Christian principles that lie behind the Church's opposition to racism**
- **how those principles can be applied to fighting racism in a church and its locality.**

You could use this format suggested by Maurice Hobbs:

We believe that ...

therefore ...

3.5 Are women treated as equals in Christianity?

Women and the priesthood

The Church of England decided in November 1992 to allow women to become priests. Revd Mother Ann Easter was one of the first women to become a priest. Revd Father Christopher Owens opposed women's ordination but has decided to abide by the democratic decision made by the Church's Parliament, the General Synod, and will remain a priest in the Church of England.

Ann and Christopher have been married for eight years.

Christopher's views

I think people have got over-excited about the priesthood. Developing the role of laypeople in the Church is much more important. I think that instead of worrying about the ordination of women we should have been encouraging other forms of leadership and service.

> On the night that the vote took place in the General Synod, we sat together in front of the television waiting for the news to come through. When it did, we both cried. Ann cried for joy. I cried with sorrow.
>
> Christopher Owens

Now the Church has become very hierarchical. Women have felt that they have to become like men, rather than celebrate their womanhood. This is a great loss to the Church.

Women have an important role to play in teaching and serving the Church. Women should also take greater responsibility in leading worship. There are existing roles open to women: the office of church warden, deacon. There were definitely women who were deacons in the Bible. The Church needs to develop these roles much more.

I do believe that there were literally 12 apostles. I also believe that Jesus deliberately set out to establish the Church with male leaders. The priesthood in my view has a 'hands-off' nature which is distinctively male.

Ann's views

Men and women are equal but different: their natures are complementary. There are aspects of priesthood which can be done better by women than men. I am thinking particularly about the caring, pastoral side of the job.

Jesus' attitude towards women was very positive. There is good evidence to suggest that the 12 disciples mentioned in the Bible were a symbol of the 12 tribes of Israel rather than the literal number of apostles. There were probably more, some of whom might well have been women. I don't think their gender is significant.

I think an all-male group of priests is odd. I would say the same of a group that was all women. I think it would limit their ability to relate to people: all the negative views of the other sex would be exaggerated.

I think that having priests who are women makes it easier for other women to feel represented. Young girls or women can see me in a procession full of men and feel that they are included.

Being a priest is no picnic! Certainly it was hard wanting to be one when I couldn't. But I have such a strong calling to be a priest, which has been supported by others, that I have no doubt about it. Being denied this vocation by others was very frustrating.

Christopher and I don't really talk about the issue. I just disagree with him but I understand what he thinks and how it is rooted in him.

Key questions for Christians

- Should men and women have different roles in the Church?
- Are men and women equal in God's sight?
- Should all women have the same roles in the Church?

The Orthodox and Catholic Churches do not ordain women as priests or ministers. Many Protestant Churches now do, although this is a subject of ongoing debate in all these traditions. Ordaining women was a fundamental change for the Church of England. Before 1992, the Church had debated the topic many times. Each time, the motion to ordain women priests had been defeated. The decisive debate in 1992 was therefore a very tense affair. You are going to have your own 'Synod' debate, using the evidence and viewpoints on pages 54–5. As you work through the text, sources and questions on these pages, add to your chart from page 54 to prepare your arguments.

Leading the opposition to women's ordination were traditionalists who said it would undermine ancient traditions. 'Anglo-Catholics' argued that if the Church of England were to ordain women then it would make relations between Anglicans and Catholics more difficult (since the Catholic Church was not in favour of women priests, see Sources C and D). Many women were content with the status quo and were active in the campaign against women's ordination. Some Evangelical Anglicans were opposed on the grounds that the Bible, which is the evangelicals' central source of authority, taught that women should not have authority in churches (see Source A, for example). Supporters of women's ordination had to find arguments against these tricky passages (see Source B, for example).

A

To the Church in Corinth

. . . As in all the churches . . . the women should keep quiet in the meetings. They are not allowed to speak; as the Jewish Law says they must not be in charge. If they want to find out about something they should ask their husbands at home. It is a disgraceful thing for a woman to speak in church.

I Corinthians 14.33–5

Saint Paul

I wonder why the churches want advice on the role of women all the time

B

To the Galatians

Through faith . . . all of you are God's children . . . So there is no difference between Jews and Gentiles, between slaves and free people, between men and women; you are all one in union with Christ Jesus.

Instructions given by Paul in Galatians 3.26–8

To my friend and helper, Timothy

. . . In every church service I want the men to pray . . . I also want the women to be modest and sensible about their clothes and to dress properly; not with fancy hair styles or with gold ornaments or pearls or expensive dresses, but with good deeds, as is proper for women who claim to be religious. Women should learn in silence and all humility. I do not allow them to teach or have authority over men; they must keep quiet. For Adam was created first, and then Eve. And it was not Adam who was deceived; it was the woman who was deceived and broke God's law . . .

I Timothy 2.8–14

1 The Galatians are confused. They have received Source B, but they have also seen Source A. They ask Paul to explain. What will they ask? What might he say?
2 How might a woman priest nowadays explain Paul's advice about the role of women?

C

At present women are involved in nearly all spheres of life: they ought to be permitted to play their part fully according to their own particular nature. It is up to everyone to see to it that women's specific and necessary participation in cultural life be acknowledged and fostered.

From *Vatican 2: Church in the Modern World*. This Council of the Catholic Church, held from 1962 from 1965, was very influential in shaping the modern Catholic Church, reinforcing doctrines and recommending stronger links with other Churches (see page 111).

DISCUSS

Imagine you are a nurse working in the geriatric ward of your local hospital. Your hospital chaplain is a woman. You have just called her to attend a dying patient. You discover he has a card like the one in Source F on his bedside table. What do you do?

D

In worship, women may:

- *read from the Bible in church, except for the gospels*
- *lead the prayers*
- *lead the singing*
- *help to explain the service*
- *act as stewards, seeing people to their seats*
- *collect money.*

Women may not:

- *be priests*
- *read the gospels out loud*
- *listen to confessions*
- *pardon sins.*

These rules apply in all situations, including in convents and schools that are women-only. A priest who is a man must be brought in where necessary.

Adapted from *Vatican 2*. This is the third instruction on the correct implementation of the constitution on the sacred liturgy, which explains how to lead Mass correctly in the Catholic tradition.

E

Angela Berners-Wilson, priest, breaks the bread during the service at St Paul's Church, Clifton, Bristol in 1994.

F

To whom it may concern

In the event of an accident or emergency where a Priest is needed please call a male Priest

One response to the decision to allow women priests

FOCUS TASK

The debate

1 **Prepare your arguments for or against the motion: 'This house supports the ordination of women as priests', using pages 54–6 to help you. So that the debate is balanced, make sure that both sides of the argument are represented. This may mean you take a different view from the one you hold.**
2 **Appoint a chairperson.**
3 **Debate the motion, making sure you write notes of other people's arguments. Then have a vote.**
4 **Compare the decision of your class with that of the General Synod in 1992. Try to account for similarities or differences in the outcome.**

The report

5 **Write an account of the debate, using your notes to help you.**

Are women and men equal in the sight of God?

In the year 584 there was a council of the Church in Mâcon, France. There was a long debate on the question, 'Are women human?' After a vote women were declared to be human by 32 votes to 31. For a long time after this many Christians believed that women had no souls and were less holy than men. Through the centuries there have been many other examples of inequality and sexism (see Sources G–I), although these attitudes are not unique to Church leaders. Others in society felt and spoke similarly.

(see Sources G–I)

ACTIVITY A

Many people would find the opinions in Sources G–I amusing but also offensive. Most Christians would agree that equality and justice are worth fighting for. Explain how these quotations from Christian men fail to treat women with either equality or justice. Why do you think they said these things? How would you respond to them?

G

Women are simple souls who like simple things, and one of the simplest is one of the simplest to give … Our family Airedale will come clear across the yard for one pat on the head. The average wife is like that. She will come across town, across the house, across the room, across to your point of view, and across almost anything to give you her love if you offer her yours with some honest approval.

Episcopal Bishop James Pike in 1968, quoted in an article in *Religion in Society*, 1985

H

Women should remain at home, sit still, keep house, and bear and bring up children … If a woman grows weary and at last dies from childbearing, it matters not. Let her die from bearing – she is there to do it.

Martin Luther, 1483–1546

I

Any woman who acts in such a way that she cannot give birth to as many children as she is capable of, makes herself guilty of that many murders.

St Augustine, sixth century CE

J

I found God within myself and I loved her passionately.

From *The Colour Purple* by Alice Walker

In many translations of the Bible the account in Genesis describes God creating 'man' in 'his' own image. The language used in this sentence has caused an argument between Christians. Not only does the original word for God have no gender, so 'his' is inappropriate, but some people feel the term 'man', meaning all human beings, does not include women. They also believe that describing God as a man implies that men are closer than women to God. People have written prayers such as Source K which attempt to redress the balance and have produced translations of the Bible using terms that include men and women, such as 'child of God' rather than 'son of God'.

Other people within the Church disagree with these arguments about language, which they say are irrelevant. They feel that feminists worry too much about minor details and forget the main beliefs of Christianity. They dislike the way that some women have changed prayers and hymns to remove 'exclusive language'. Nor are they comfortable with new writing which uses feminine words and images. The 'inclusive language' edition of the New International Version Bible comes with a 'money-back' guarantee for people who do not like it!

ACTIVITY B

Read Janet Morley's prayer (Source K) to ten people and note down their responses. What conclusions do you draw from your findings?

K

God our Mother,
You hold our life within you,
nourish us at your breast,
and teach us to walk alone.
Help us so to receive your tenderness
and respond to your challenge
that others may draw life from us,
in your name.

Janet Morley in the *SPCK Book of Christian Prayer*

L

Traditional women or modern women?

M

I don't feel that God is calling women to be in charge. Generally we don't want to be bothered with all the hassle and responsibility of leadership. I enjoy the contribution I make to my local church. When my own children were small I needed to take them out of the service, so it was no bother to look after other people's children as well. I've just carried on ever since. I wouldn't want to stand up and speak in front of other people. I don't feel confident enough to do it and I'd rather leave it to those who do.

I like the church the way it is. I wouldn't change it. I enjoy all the old hymns and the beauty of the traditional language. I know it includes me when they say 'men' and I think God treats me the same as everyone else. I'd feel funny trying to pray to a woman.

Miriam, a housewife and a mother, runs the crèche in her local church.

N

Women have been ministers in the United Reformed Church ever since it began in 1972. I thought seriously about becoming one while I was at university but decided against it, and I have no regrets. I find teaching rewarding and I feel able to take responsibility within my Church in other ways.

I regularly lead the prayers of intercession in church and I read the lesson. I help distribute the bread and the wine during Communion and very occasionally I preach the sermon. As an elder I have responsibility for 20 members of the congregation. I try to visit everyone at least once a year or invite them to my house. I am there for them if they need my support. I attend Church meetings, where all the important business in the life of our Church is discussed, and have an equal vote.

I do feel that men dominate the key roles in the Church and women need to be better represented. I don't enjoy sexist hymns and I sing different words if they fit, although I wouldn't be prepared to force other people to do this if they didn't want to. I enjoy reading women's religious writing and I particularly admire Janet Morley's work. I was not brought up to think of God as Mother but I am developing my ideas and beliefs.

Emily, a teacher and an elder in the URC

ACTIVITY

You have beeen asked to set up a Christian Women of the Year award.

1 **Devise some criteria for the award.**
2 **Write a nomination for a woman you particularly admire. Explain:**
   a) **who they are**
   b) **what they have done**
   c) **why you admire them.**
   You could nominate any of the women on these two pages, or another woman.

DISCUSS

1 **Some Christians find the sculpture in Source Q a helpful image of Jesus. Others find it offensive.**
   a) **Try to explain why they can hold such different views.**
   b) **Explain your own view of this statue.**

O

Diana, Princess of Wales and Mother Teresa of Calcutta died in the same week in 1997. As well as being world famous, they were also celebrated for their caring roles. They had great respect for each other's work. Mother Teresa was best known for her work with street children, orphans and lepers. Princess Diana was particularly associated with the plight of victims of landmines and with AIDS sufferers. Do you think that Mother Teresa and Princess Diana are modern or traditional women?

P

[Mary's] story is an anchor for my faith. I keep coming back to the fact that she was the first person to receive a resurrection appearance, that she was called to become an apostle to the apostles. I have a deep conviction that the present treatment of women does not reflect the mind of Jesus. Mary Magdalene's story of faithful discipleship gives me courage, and I resolve again that I will not give up.

Carlene, a Catholic, commenting on the story in John 20.11–18 where Mary Magdalene is the first person to see Jesus after the resurrection, quoted in *Women at the Well*

Q

The statue of Christa in the church of St John the Divine, New York, USA

FOCUS TASK

1   Read Source P. When Carlene says she draws the strength 'not to give up' what problems do you think she means?

2   The following stories are meetings between Jesus and three different women:
- John 4.5–30
- John 8.1–11
- Mark 14.3–9.

Read them and write as many words as you can to describe Jesus' attitude towards these women.

3   Now write an essay to explain how far you agree with Carlene that the 'present treatment of women does not reflect the mind of Jesus'.
You could use this structure:
a) an introduction explaining why this issue concerns many people today
b) a paragraph explaining the ways in which discrimination against women is being challenged in the Church
c) a paragraph explaining the ways in which the Church discriminates against women
d) a paragraph summarising Jesus' attitude to women
e) your conclusion as to how far this attitude is reflected in current attitudes in the Church.

3.6 How can Christians serve others?

Serve those in need...

Serving others had been an important part of Jesus' message. The first Christians were well known for the way they looked after other Christians and those in need. Tertullian, a North African Church Leader living in the third century CE, wrote 'Every man once a month brings some modest coin – or whenever he wishes, and only if he does wish ... they are not spent on banquets ... but to feed the poor and to bury them, for boys and girls who lack property and parents, and then for slaves grown old and ship-wrecked mariners: and any who may be in mines, islands or prisons, provided that it is for the sake of God's school.'

A

At the Final Judgement the King will divide peoples of all nations into two groups: those that served others and those that did not.

He will say to the righteous:
'Come and possess the kingdom which has been prepared for you, for
I was hungry and you fed me,
Thirsty and you gave me a drink;
I was a stranger and you received me in your homes,
Naked and you clothed me;
I was sick and you took care of me,
In prison and you visited me;
The righteous will ask, 'When did we do all these things?'
The King will reply, 'I tell you, whenever you did this for the least important of these brothers and sisters of mine, you did it for me.'

Adapted from Matthew 25.31–46

C

Volunteers helping the homeless for 'Crisis at Christmas'

B

Make us worthy, Lord, to serve our fellows through the world who live and die in poverty and hunger. Give them, through our hands, this day their daily bread, and, by our understanding, love, peace and joy.

Non-Christians and Christians both do social work, but... we do it for someone. We do it for God. It is our love of God in action.

Two statements by Mother Teresa (1910–97), who founded a Catholic order of nuns who work among the poor in India and around the world

D

Christ has no body now on earth but yours, no hands but yours, no feet but yours. Yours are the eyes through which Christ's compassion is to look out on the world. Yours are the feet with which he is doing good. Yours are the hands with which he is to bless others now.

St Teresa of Avila, writing more than 400 years ago

ACTIVITY

1   Using Sources A–D draw up two lists: 'Reasons to serve others' and 'Ways of serving others'. You can also find many other examples throughout this book of Christians serving others.

2   There's more to serving others than 'doing good'. Explain how each of these decisions might allow a Christian to serve others:
a) how to vote at an election
b) deciding what job to do
c) whether to marry and how to raise a family
d) what to buy in shops
e) what organisations to give money or time to.

1 **On your own, complete the following sentences. You could get ideas from Source E.**
 • I obey … because …
 • I respect … because …
 • … are authority figures in my life because …

2 **Compare your answers with someone else's and see if you can identify any common reasons for obeying or respecting certain authority figures.**

3 **Do you think Source F contains good advice for a Christian? Give reasons for your answer.**

And respect authority …

E

God's authority versus government authority

Christians distinguish between sacred authority (authority that comes from God) and secular authority (authority that comes from human institutions).

Jesus himself was often in conflict with religious and political authorities, as were the first Christians. Paul and Peter gave almost identical advice for such situations.

F

Secular authority

Everyone must obey the state authorities, because no authority exists without God's permission, and the existing authorities have been put there by God.

Paul in Romans 13.1

Sacred authority

If an authority is doing things that are against the teaching of Jesus then, 'We must obey God, not men.'

Peter in Acts 5.29

Both Paul and Peter acted on this and disobeyed Jewish and Roman authorities when they felt their faith was being challenged. It is likely that Peter was eventually executed for it.

For Paul and Peter, the distinction between sacred and secular was very clear. The government was not Christian, in fact it was strongly anti-Christian. However, in Britain today the distinction between sacred and secular authority is more blurred. For example, through their place in the House of Lords, some Church of England Bishops have a vote on all new laws being introduced by the government. And the Queen is head of the Church of England and of the government. But does this mean that all laws in Britain are God's will? Not many Christians think so! In some countries this is an even greater dilemma.

FOCUS TASK

1 **Working in groups of three, devise a situation in which a Christian faces a conflict between the demands of their religious beliefs and their government. One is telling them to do one thing, the other is telling them the opposite. You can get ideas from earlier in this book, for example page 23, but ask your teacher if you need help finding ideas.**

2 **Work in your group to draw up guidelines for resolving conflicts between different authorities.**

Liberation Theology

In some situations the Christian principle 'serve others' comes directly into conflict with the principle of 'obey your government'. One dramatic example of this in recent years comes from the experience of Latin-American Christians.

In the 1960s many countries in Latin America were military dictatorships. These regimes were often brutal and corrupt. They ignored basic human rights, took the best land and industries for their own profit, murdered their own citizens, and followed economic policies that made the poorest poorer and the richest richer. A tiny minority lived in luxury, while the vast majority lived in abject poverty. Anyone who questioned the rulers was branded a communist and was likely to be killed.

It was very difficult for Christians in these countries to believe that the government was (to use the words in Source F) 'put there by God'.

It was equally difficult to see how Christians in these countries could serve others without also challenging the government.

The situation of poor people has not changed much, but out of this situation developed a way of thinking about God and religion which became known as Liberation Theology. This sees God as a liberator who sets people free, who sides with the poor, who hates injustice.

G

The spirit of the Lord is upon me, because he has chosen me to bring good news to the poor. He has sent me to proclaim liberty for the captives and recovery of sight to the blind; to set free the oppressed, and announce that the time has come when the Lord will save his people.

Luke 4.18–19, in which Jesus begins his public ministry by quoting the Old Testament prophet Isaiah

H

Jesus is God, Man and Woman standing in firm solidarity … This is a God who is sensitive to suffering. The discovery of a God who is in pilgrimage with the people is a discovery which gives meaning to their struggle and makes everyday life bearable in the midst of oppression.

Luz Beatriz Arellano, a Nicaraguan Christian and feminist

I

When you made this universe at the beginning of time; you wanted a world where the strong did not oppress the weak, where injustice did not conquer truth, where rich and poor shared their food equally. But we confess, O God, that we have turned your beautiful creation into a world of corruption and death, where the poor are oppressed and justice is crushed. Forgive us, God, and teach us how to live according to your wishes. Amen.

A Latin-American prayer

J

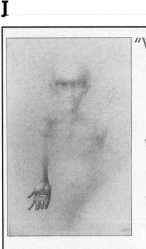

"When I give food to the poor, they call me a saint.

When I ask why the poor have no food, they call me a communist."

– Dom Helder Camara

Helder Camara is a Brazilian Catholic theologian and priest. He has been a champion of the poor and of non-violent social change in Brazil, and worldwide, through *Vatican 2* (see page 111).

1 Write three ways in which you think that a Christian saying the prayer in Source I could back it up with practical action.
2 Use the information on this page to explain in your own words the message of Source J.
3 Read the story strip on the opposite page. Just before his death, Romero said that 'Killing priests was good news.' What do you think he meant?

What about Britain?

Governments do not expect to be criticised or attacked by the Church – even in a supposedly mature democracy with freedom of speech, such as Britain. In 1985 the Church of England published a report on 'Faith in the City', which in parts criticised the Conservative government of the day for having policies that were not helping the poor in our society. Margaret Thatcher (Prime Minister at that time) reacted by saying that it was wrong for the Church to involve itself in politics and that the Church should be more worried about spiritual and moral leadership.

K The life and death of Oscar Romero

FOCUS TASK

'The Church's primary role must be a spiritual one. I say this as a member of the Anglican Church.'
Lord Jenkins of Roding, former Conservative MP

'You cannot apply the truth of God without being political.'
Roger Forster, evangelical Christian leader

1 Which speaker do you agree with more? Explain why.
2 How does a Christian decide what is unjust and what is simply unpopular?
3 'Religious believers have more responsibility than other people to protest against injustice in society.' Do you agree? Give reasons for your opinion, showing that you have thought about more than one point of view.

Relationships – Review tasks

A

1 What happened in the Church of England in 1992 to make this illustration topical?
2 Explain why both sides in the debate felt as they did.
3 List three other examples of perceived inequality in society.
4 Choose one of your examples and explain what Christians might do to combat such inequality.
5 In Galatians 3.28, Paul says that all 'are one in union with Christ Jesus.' Do you agree?
Give reasons.

B

1 Imagine that a Christian priest or minister is invited to talk to a church youth club about sex. Explain two teachings from the Bible that she might use in her talk.
2 Some young Christians pledge to wait until they marry to have sex. Explain why they might do this.
3 'Christian churches should refuse to marry people who have had a sexual relationship before their wedding day.' Do you agree? Give reasons for your answer showing that you have considered other points of view.

C

1 Explain what St Paul taught about relationships between
a) husbands and wives
b) parents and children
in his letter to the Ephesians (Ephesians 5.21-6.4).
2 Choose 1a) or 1b) and explain why this advice might be controversial today.
3 Explain, with examples, how Christians might support families in modern society who are faced with difficult family relationships.

D

'Christian teaching on relationships is irrelevant and out of date!' Explain whether you agree with this statement, showing that you have considered other points of view. Refer to examples from pages 33-63.

An illustration that appeared in *Private Eye* magazine in 1992

UNIT 4

Global issues

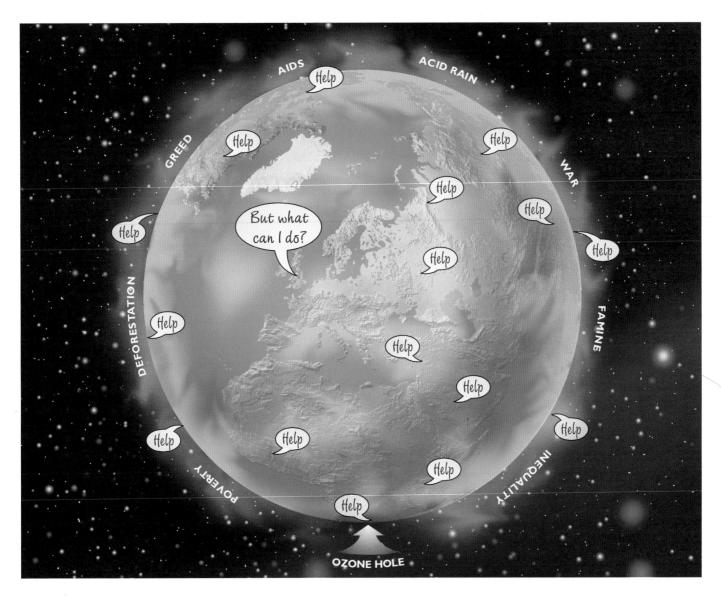

This cartoon shows a number of world issues.

- Are there any issues you would want to add?
- Which of the problems in this cartoon do you think is the most serious?
- Which do you feel you can do something about?

4.1 How can individuals change the world?

A

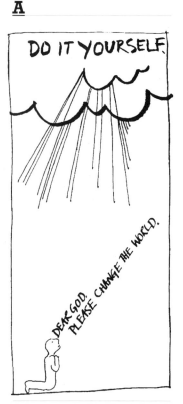

The problems of the world are beamed onto our televisions every day and many people feel helpless when faced by them. However, we are probably not as helpless as we think we are! It is possible, with the communications available through travel, trade, media and information technology, to influence the world for the better. Now that such global issues (see page 65) are so well known, they have become part of our everyday morality. Decisions we make today can affect some of these issues! This unit investigates some of these issues and Christian responses to them.

ACTIVITY

B

You are walking home from school and you pass a toddler drowning in a shallow canal. There are two people fishing – apparently unaware of the problem. You know you can save the child at no risk to yourself – although it will mean getting wet. **What do you do?**

C

You are reading a newspaper and you find an advertisement asking you for money. It says that £10 can save the life of a child by providing clean water. You have more than £10 pocket money saved up, which you were intending to spend on a new **CD**. **What do you do?**

1 Do you think that there are any similarities between these two situations?
2 What is the appropriate Christian response in each case?
3 Do you agree with the message of Source A?

4.2 How should Christians use their money?

1 **Why do you think the young woman in Source A chose the minister's house?**

2 **Do you think the minister was right to turn the young woman away? Give reasons.**

A

One cold evening in winter, a young woman knocked on our door. She was covered in a blanket and shivering. She begged my father, the local minister, for enough money to get to a hostel by bus. He refused, as he refused all people who came to our house because he was worried that if word got around, every tramp and vagrant in the local area would be running to our front door. My mum once let someone in for bread and soup. Dad was really cross when he found out.

What does the Bible teach about money?

If Christians look to the Bible for guidance on this question they will find a lot of teaching about money.

In fact, there is more teaching about money, wealth and poverty in the Bible than there is about supposedly 'religious' subjects such as heaven or hell. Source B refers you to some of the central teachings. There are hundreds more references, which can be interpreted in very different ways. Christians might claim they are following Jesus' example, whatever their point of view.

Christ expels the money-changers from the temple (John 2.13–16) by Edward Burra (1905–76)

B

THE BIBLE AND MONEY

Matthew 6.19–21

Luke 16.19–31

Luke 21.1–4

Matthew 14.15–21

Matthew 19.16–22

1 Timothy 6.6–10

2 Corinthians 8.1–15

Acts 2.44–7

Leviticus 25.14, 23, 35–6

Matthew 19.23–4

Key questions for Christians

- Is my money my own or God's?
- Should Christians be rich?
- Are inequality and poverty a part of God's plan for the world?
- How can Christians fight poverty?

ACTIVITY

Work in groups.

Each take one or two passages from **Source B** and fill out your own copy of the chart below. If each person in your group chooses different passages, you should manage to complete the chart by sharing your information. We have filled out the first row as an example.

Passage	Whose teaching is this?	What does it say about money	Christian responses	My view
Matthew 6.19–21	Jesus	Do not allow your life to revolve around money because you cannot take it with you when you die.	Do not get depressed if you have no money. Give money to charity if you have some.	I agree/ disagree because . . .

Should Christians be rich?

> Yes, if they use their wealth wisely and well.

Case study 1: Sir John Templeton

Sir John Templeton grew up on a farm in Tennessee in the USA. He completed a successful education at Yale and Oxford Universities. Then he started a business as a financial consultant on Wall Street in New York.

Even when Sir John was at his poorest he chose to give away ten per cent of everything that he earned – a practice known as 'tithing'. Through his natural talent and careful management of his money he became a very wealthy man. Until 1992 Sir John ran a multi-million dollar group of investment companies. He helped other people to invest their money in order to increase their wealth. He managed funds for over 2 million investors worldwide. In 1992 he sold his businesses for $400 million.

Sir John combines his business interests with his Christian faith. He started the Templeton Prize in 1972, to be awarded for progress in religion. This prize is now worth more money than the Nobel Peace Prize. Sir John gives money to support projects around the world that further our understanding of spirituality and the importance of human character. He believes that there are good ideals in all religions and cultures, which should be followed to make the world a better place.

John Templeton was knighted by Queen Elizabeth II in 1987 for 'services to philanthropy' (i.e. caring for humankind).

C

D

The most important thing in human life is to seek and do the will of God. A person who does this is living by faith. He or she doesn't have to look around trying to find faith; it springs from within.

From *Discovering the Laws of Life* by John Templeton, a collection of sayings about how to get the best from life from a spiritual perspective

1 **If Sir John Templeton thinks money is not important, why has he made so much of it?**

2 **Using wealth wisely and well is called 'good stewardship'. What evidence is there that Sir John Templeton is a 'good steward'.**

3 **Do you approve of the way he has chosen to spend his money? Explain your answer. Suggest causes you would support if you were Sir John.**

4 **'Money cannot buy happiness'. Do you think this is true? Give more than one point of view.**

E

Week 14

'If you would find gold you must seek where gold is' William Juneau

We see people every day searching in the wrong places for the things they desire. Too many of our fellow humans try to find peace and happiness in drugs, alcohol and sensual excitement, but they don't find what they want because they are searching in the wrong place. If you want peace, the first place to look is within yourself. It's not an external condition so much as an internal one.

If you want the company of good people, try going to the places where good people go – churches, charity functions, community picnics. Good people will not be found where gangsters and thieves hang out.

Those in search of an easier, softer way to obtain the important things of life often find cheap imitations or nothing at all. The miner who searches for gold on the beach because the digging is easy will certainly find lots of sand, but he'll never find gold. Sometimes we must dig amongst stones and hard clay to find the treasure we seek. And when we do we will know our efforts have not been wasted.

From *Discovering the Laws of Life* by John Templeton

C̲ase study 2: The Iona Community

> No, wealth and possessions should be shared.

F

SCOTLAND

Iona —

In 1938 George MacLeod founded a Christian community on the tiny island of Iona off the west coast of Scotland.

Clergymen and helpers gave up time and money to learn building, carpentry and stone-masonry, and together they rebuilt Iona's ruined abbey.

The George MacLeod Centre was later opened to provide a place where young people from across the world could come and live for a time in a community. They contribute to practical tasks like cleaning, cooking and gardening. In the summer volunteers look after visitors as guides or shop-workers. When they are not working they follow a regular pattern of worship and study as well as enjoying the company of other people within the community.

The people who live in the community do so because they believe that a life shared with others is better than one where people are on their own as individuals or in small family clusters. Community members come from all walks of life and are drawn to Iona for personal or spiritual reasons. Their life is relatively simple. No one is really rich in material possessions but no one has to endure real poverty.

The Iona Community does not just worry about its own affairs. Most Community members live and work away from Iona, in deprived areas of Scotland. Some support Church of Scotland projects in the poorest parts of Glasgow. Others are at work in the wider world. These members of the Community return to Iona for one week per year. They give a proportion of their income to the Community. The Iona Community has led anti-nuclear protests and campaigns against what they regard as unjust government policies. Worship in the Iona Community focuses on social concerns around the world. This is reflected in daily prayers, such as Source G.

5 **How would you like living in a community, sharing everything you owned?**

6 **How likely is it that shared possessions would make some people in the community lazy?**

7 **The Iona Community does much to support poor people both in this country and abroad. Which do you think should be their priority as Christians – home or abroad?**

8 **What effect do you think prayers like Source G have?**

Explain your answers to these questions.

G

Here is a gaping sore, Lord:
half the world diets,
the other half hungers;
half the world is housed,
the other half homeless;
half the world pursues profit,
the other half senses loss.
Redeem our souls, redeem our peoples,
redeem our times.

A prayer by John Bell, of the Iona Community from the *SPCK Book of Christian Prayer*

FOCUS TASK

In 1992 Sir John Templeton presented the Iona Community with one of his prestigious UK awards. Imagine you are Sir John's assistant. Draft a letter congratulating the Iona Community and explaining why they won. Try to refer to how Iona has applied some of the Bible teaching you summarised on page 67.

We believe in life before death

H

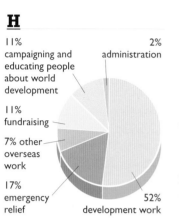

11%
campaigning and
educating people
about world
development

2%
administration

11%
fundraising

7% other
overseas
work

17%
emergency
relief

52%
development work

How Christian Aid spends
its money

SAVE AS ...

Using the example of the
Deccan Development
Society, explain in your
own words the difference
between:
a) disaster relief
b) development work.

How does Christian Aid fight poverty?

Christian Aid was formed in Britain and Ireland as the Second World War was coming to an end. It was set up to help refugees and churches recover from the aftermath of war. Gradually the work of the organisation grew to include countries from around the world. Over 40 Churches in the United Kingdom and Ireland are now part of Christian Aid. Its income is around £40 million. This is raised through fundraising activity, such as door-to-door collection in Christian Aid Week and through donations from member Churches, supporters and the general public.

Development work = helping the poor to help themselves

Although Christian Aid occasionally provides disaster-relief, helping when emergencies happen, only a small part of its income is used in this way. The bulk of its work is in 'development work' (see Source H) – long-term, small-scale projects run locally. These development projects help people to help themselves, to avoid spending their lives constantly dependent on help from outside. This is known as SUSTAINABLE development.

Christian Aid is involved in many aspects of development work: improving health and sanitation, including population control; protecting the rights of refugees; fighting for greater democracy and freedom for ordinary people; improving standards of literacy and numeracy in countries where education opportunities are limited.

Many denominations have chosen to support the work of Christian Aid rather than set up their own rival world development agencies. The United Reformed Church, for example, has chosen to support four Christian Aid projects as part of its 'Commitment for Life' programme. One of these projects is the Deccan Development Society (the DDS) in Central South India (see Source I). Once financial help and legal advice have been given to initiate the project, Christian Aid expects the DDS to run itself and be self-financing. Christian Aid does not provide foreign experts or expensive modern technology. This is inappropriate. Development work needs to build the skills and power of the local people.

I

1 2

Anishama in the village of Indoor. She is teaching members of the local women's sangham (council) about new farming methods which can produce more food and reduce environmental damage. In I she is demonstrating how to contour the land to prevent erosion.

J

Action request
from Christian Aid

Please send off the enclosed postcards

"The debt burden is killing people because they cannot afford to go to hospital. If they don't have drugs they die. This is a direct result of the debt crisis."

Dear Ambassador

This year is the 45th anniversary of the London Agreement, when Germany benefited from debt cancellation. In view of this, I am disappointed at the German government's reluctance to support measures that would provide sustainable debt relief for the poorest countries in the world.

I recognise that Germany has taken some steps to cancel the bilateral debt of a number of poor countries. But with millions more people still suffering from the effects of debt, more has to be done.

Please reconsider your position on international debt relief and use your influence to ensure that it is on the agenda and discussed in May by the G8.

Yours sincerely

Name:

Address:

follow-up action ▷▷▷▷▷▷▷▷▷▷▷▷▷▷▷▷▷▷▷▷▷▷▷▷▷▷▷

▶ **Send a pound coin to the new Chancellor,** to repeat Christian Aid's message to the new Government.

▶ **Stick your pound to a card or letter.** Say this is a symbol of your desire for the backlog of unjust Third World debt to be cancelled.

▶ **Say that now he is in a position of major influence on the international stage,** you hope he will make sure Britain sets a shining example to the rest of the world.

Send it in an envelope to: The Chancellor of the Exchequer, 11 Downing Street, London SW1A 2AJ.

Extracts from Christian Aid's *Action Request*, February 1998 and *Action News*, July 1997

1 **Source J shows two examples of Christian Aid's campaigns. Which campaign do you think would be more likely to succeed? Why?**

2 **Why does Christian Aid feel a responsibility to fight for the prawn farmers (Sources K and L)?**

3 **How do workers for Christian Aid follow the example of Jesus? Think about:**
   • **his teaching**
   • **his example.**

Campaigns = changing the policies that hold back the poor

Christian Aid argues that poverty is often caused, or made worse, by government policies in Britain and other developed countries. For example, in past decades Western governments and banks lent billions of pounds to developing countries who cannot now repay the debts. The interest they have to pay on these debts drains wealth from the developing countries. So Christian Aid and other development agencies campaign for such debts to be cancelled. Christian Aid also argues that alleviating poverty requires changing patterns of trade and encourages its supporters to join the fight for fairer trade. However, some Christians worry about such policies, which they feel are too 'political'. Christian Aid would not deny they are political; they would agree with Roger Forster (see page 63) that applying Christianity in these situations means being political. However, Christian Aid is not party-political. It calls on all parties to support policies which help alleviate poverty.

One recent issue which has involved Christian Aid is the prawn trade. A 1996 report claimed that land along the South Indian coast was being damaged by intensive prawn farming. It was alleged that local farmers were losing land to bigger, more powerful companies.

K

It is possible to produce 'fairly traded' prawns, cultivated without upsetting the environment and impoverishing local people. Importers and retailers should seek out prawns from sustainable sources, and commit themselves to a code of good practice based on Christian Aid's model. The World Bank and other funding agencies should support only small-scale, traditional cultivation in which prawns are often produced in rotation with other crops. Third World governments should stop intensive methods which are blighting the lives of some of their poorest people.

From *After the Prawn Rush: the human and environmental costs of commercial prawn farming* by Kevan Bundell and Eileen Maybin, May 1996

L

They tell us our country needs the foreign currency generated by commercial prawn farming. But we certainly don't need the environmental devastation and social division these farms are causing. We don't want to make our traditional rice growers and fishing communities hungry and destitute. We see no new schools or hospitals for our rural villages as a result of these prawn farms. Where is all the profit going? Not to the people whose land is being taken but to the fat-cat investors who bleed us dry and then move on.

Khushi Kabir, campaigner, also from *After the Prawn Rush*

✓ CHECKPOINT

Why do Christians help the poor?

All Christian traditions would agree that it is a Christian duty to help the poor. Many different sources of authority point Christians towards this responsibility. For example:

The Bible. Much of the Old Testament law is designed to protect the poor. The Old Testament prophets call for justice and compassion for the poor. In the New Testament, Jesus loves the poor and has compassion for them. He praises those who help the poor; he condemns those who do nothing for them (see Source A on page 60, for example). Much of Jesus' teaching is concerned with stewardship. The good steward is one who uses what they have been given or what they have earned wisely or well. Using wealth wisely and well, according to Jesus, means using it to show compassion.

Church teaching. All traditions emphasise the need to help the poor. At the most obvious level, they give money to agencies that help the poor, or set up such agencies. More importantly, they fight for justice for the poor. For example, as part of the influential *Vatican 2* (see page 111) the Catholic Church decided that it should be closely involved with poor people's struggle for justice. *Vatican 2* sent a signal from the Catholic leadership that allowed the Liberation Theology movement to develop in Catholic communities around the world (see page 62).

Christian leaders. Some of the most widely respected Christian leaders of the past and present are those most closely identified with helping the poor, such as Desmond Tutu in South Africa, Mother Teresa in India and Martin Luther King in the USA (see pages 50 and 60). The example and teaching of others inspires Christians to try to help the poor.

Individual conscience. This is a powerful motivation to help the poor. Christians may be moved to action by hearing the story of an ordinary human being struggling in poverty. Their conscience stimulates them to take action.

ACTIVITY A

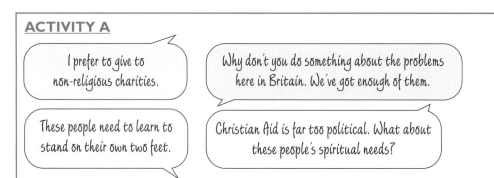

> I prefer to give to non-religious charities.

> Why don't you do something about the problems here in Britain. We've got enough of them.

> These people need to learn to stand on their own two feet.

> Christian Aid is far too political. What about these people's spiritual needs?

Study the statements above. These were reasons given for not supporting Christian Aid during a door-to-door collection. How would you respond? Explain your answer with reference to:

a) **the information about Christian Aid**

b) **Christian beliefs about money and helping the poor (try to refer to Bible passages you looked at on page 67)**

c) **your own beliefs.**

You could role play a conversation on the doorstep.

ACTIVITY B

Does it matter that some Christians spend lots of money on themselves while other Christians in the world are poor? Refer to more than one point of view in your answer.

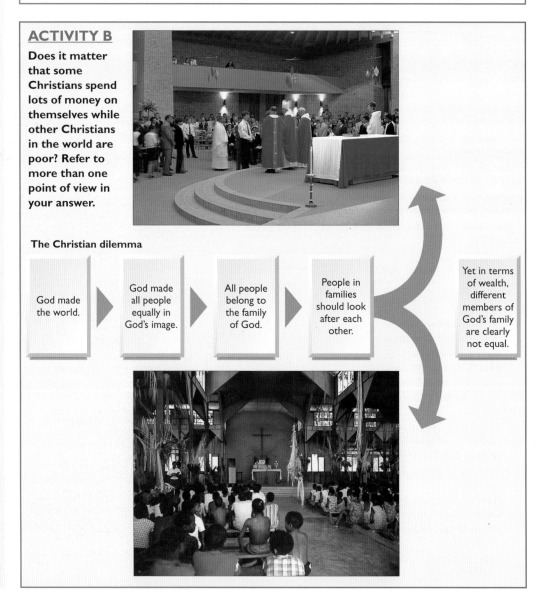

The Christian dilemma

God made the world. → God made all people equally in God's image. → All people belong to the family of God. → People in families should look after each other. → Yet in terms of wealth, different members of God's family are clearly not equal.

SAVE AS ...

Look back to Source A on page 67.

1 Do you regard this woman as poor?
2 In the light of your work on this unit, write a summary of how a Christian could decide whether and how to help this woman.

Poverty or inequality?

At a European Union meeting, it was recently claimed that there was no longer any poverty in Britain, there was simply inequality. Do you agree? Many people would agree. Others would disagree. It all depends how you define poverty. Does poverty mean to be starving? Or does it mean to struggle to pay your mortgage?

In Britain today we are aware of people begging for food and money. There are many homeless people. Some people fall through the welfare 'safety net' and literally own only the possessions they can carry with them. They are dependent on other people's gifts for food. Are they really poor? Or are they just poorer than other people?

FOCUS TASK

1 Explain why some Christians might wish to have this stained glass window in their church.
2 Explain why others might not think it appropriate.
3 Describe how Christian Aid is helping to combat the problems of world poverty.

Either:

4 Work in a group to draw designs for a series of stained glass windows to go alongside Source M, showing:
a) other problems of poverty
b) possible Christian action to overcome poverty.

Or:

5 With your group, draw up a set of at least five guidelines for all Christians to help them decide how to use their money. Support each guideline with reference to a passage from the Bible.

M

A stained glass window in St Mary's Church, Bishop Auckland, County Durham

4.3   Responsible stewards or plundering idiots?

This is Bonsall ...

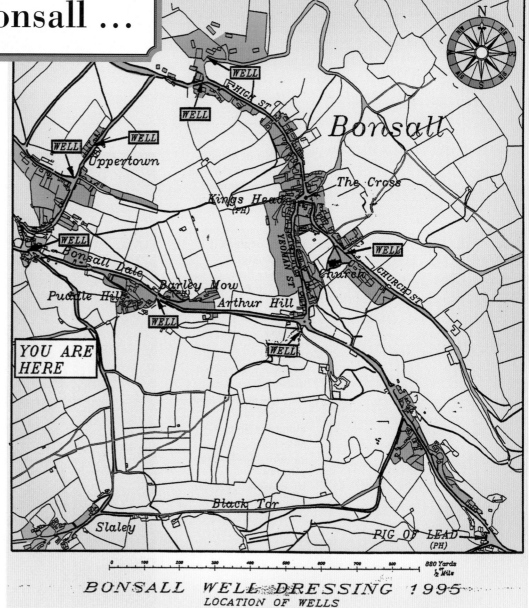

BONSALL WELL DRESSING 1995
LOCATION OF WELLS

'My mother often helps to make the Methodist Chapel well-dressing at the end of our road. She uses flowers from our garden. This year the theme was "journeys" and our picture was of Jesus calming the storm. It was based on a reading from Luke 8.24.'

'People round the village chose different journeys, some religious, some not. In Uppertown the children made a well-dressing of the Apollo XI Moon landing. Another well had a picture of the Kontiki expedition to the South Pacific. St James' Anglican Church based their dressing on the Sermon on the Mount.'

'Wells' week unites the whole village, Christians and non-Christians. People from all different backgrounds work together to make it a special and happy occasion.'

'All the wells in the village are blessed by the local vicar in a special Sunday service. We sing hymns and say a prayer at each well. At some we listen to a reading from the Bible. We also try to collect money from visitors. This goes to support a charity, often connected with children.'

'Wells' week is one of the most exciting weeks of the year. We have a carnival through the village with competitions and prizes. This year we had a sheep roast and Karaoke night in the park on Saturday night! All week there are special activities: traditional dancing, treasure hunts, flower and craft festivals and even hen races!'

DISCUSS
To what extent is well-dressing a Christian custom? Give more than one point of view.

…ALL THE WELLS IN THE PLACE ARE DECORATED WITH WREATHS AND GARLANDS OF FRESH GATHERED FLOWERS. BOARDS ARE USED AND COVERED WITH MOIST CLAY INTO WHICH THE STEMS OF THE FLOWERS ARE SET TO FORM A BEAUTIFUL MOSAIC WORK. THE BOARDS ARE PLACED IN THE SPRING SO THAT THE WATER APPEARS TO ISSUE FROM THEM. VILLAGERS PUT ON THEIR BEST ATTIRE AND OPEN THEIR HOUSES TO THEIR FRIENDS. THERE IS A SERVICE AT THE CHURCH WHERE A SERMON IS PREACHED. A PROCESSION TAKES PLACE WHEN THE WELLS ARE VISITED IN TURN. THE PSALMS FOR THE DAY, A LETTER AND A GOSPEL ARE READ AT EACH WELL. THE WHOLE FINISHES WITH A HYMN SUNG BY THE CHURCH SINGERS ACCOMPANIED BY A BAND. THE REMAINDER OF THE DAY IS SPENT IN RURAL SPORTS AND HOLIDAY PASTIMES …

Adapted from Glover's *History of Derby*, 1829

'Nobody is sure how well-dressing began. Some like to think it dates back to the times of the Great Plague in England. Then pure, clean water was literally a gift of life! Others say that the Celts and the Ancient Greeks used to decorate water springs with flowers as a sign of respect to the gods.'

'Nowadays we like to dress wells because it's a bit of fun. But also it gives us a chance to worship God as the Creator of the world. We give thanks for the water that sustains our lives and the beautiful flowers and trees in our gardens.'

ACTIVITY A

In groups, imagine you are villagers in Bonsall. Using the information above, plan next year's well-dressing week. You should aim to repeat successes and add new ideas of your own. Remember that this is an opportunity to celebrate the environment as well as to have fun.

ACTIVITY B

Think of aspects of your local environment for which you are grateful. You could focus on your school or your local area.

Organise a celebration of one or more of these aspects. Think about appropriate decorations and rituals. You might want to make this an opportunity to raise money for a relevant charity.

Key questions for Christians

- Why are there environmental problems?
- What are a Christian's environmental rights and responsibilities?
- Who does the world belong to?

The Christian belief in God's gift of Creation

Christians believe that God created the world. The Creation story (Source A) is fundamental to a Christian view of the world. It contains three important ideas that affect Christians' attitudes to the environment:

Worship – The natural world is God's work and is to be celebrated and enjoyed. Celebrating the natural world is an important part of Christian worship, both for individual Christians (see Source C, for example) and groups of Christians praying and singing about it, for example at harvest festivals or well-dressings.

Interdependence – Human beings are part of God's Creation. All parts of creation are interdependent and are linked to all other parts. So any damage to a part of creation is damaging to us (see Source B).

Stewardship – Human beings are given a special responsibility within creation: to control it, cultivate it and guard it – to be 'good stewards'. A steward is someone who carefully looks after something that is not theirs. They look after it to the best of their ability for whoever really owns it – in this case, God. Some have interpreted the Creation story as giving people a right to exploit the environment. Most Christians would disagree with this.

In Genesis 1 and 2 rights are balanced against responsibilities. Later in the Bible, God gives very specific instructions about what we would now regard as responsible environmental stewardship, for example in Exodus 23.10–11 and Deuteronomy 20.19–20.

A

So God created human beings, making them to be like himself. He created them male and female, blessed them, and said, 'Have many children, so that your descendants will live all over the earth and bring it under their control. I am putting you in charge of the fish, the birds, and all the wild animals. I have provided all kinds of grain and all kinds of fruit for you to eat; but for all the wild animals and for all the birds I have provided grass and leafy plants for food' – and it was done ... The Lord God placed the man in the garden of Eden to cultivate it and guard it.

Genesis 1.27–30, 2.15

1 **'All things bright and beautiful' is often sung in primary schools. Should children be encouraged to sing it? Why?**

B

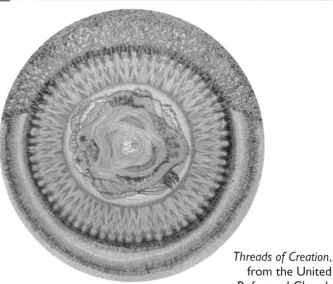

Threads of Creation, from the United Reformed Church

C

*Glory be to God for dappled things –
for skies of couple-colour as a brinded cow;
For rose-moles all in stipple upon trout that swim;
Fresh-firecoal chestnut falls; finches' wings;
Landscape plotted and pierced-fold, fallow and plough;
And all trades, their gear and tackle and trim.*

*All things counter, original, spare, strange;
Whatever is fickle, freckled (who knows how?)
With swift, slow; sweet, sour: adazzle, dim;
He fathers-forth whose beauty is past change:
Praise him.*

Catholic poet Gerard Manley Hopkins, 1844–89

SAVE AS ...

1 Copy the diagram below and complete it with reference to Source A.
2 Draw another similar diagram and complete it with reference to either Matthew 6.28–9 or Exodus 23.10–11.

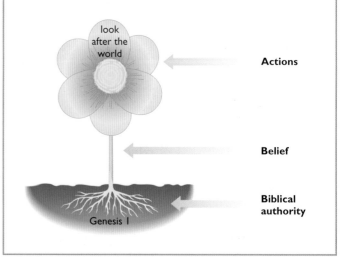

Environmental rights or environmental responsibilities?

The world has moved on since the days of Adam and Eve! Many human beings have been able to enjoy the world. Unfortunately they have not always taken care of the environment. Some Christians are aware of this and are trying to help people balance their rights and responsibilities better.

D

Creator of Earth
and of all Earth's children,
Creator of soil and sea and sky
and the tapestries of stars,
we turn to you for guidance
as we look on our mutilated planet,
and pray it is not too late
for us to rescue our wounded world.
We have been so careless.
We have failed to nurture the fragile life
you entrusted to our keeping.
We beg you for forgiveness
and we ask you to begin again.
Be with us in our commitment to Earth.
Let all the Earth say: Amen.

A prayer by Miriam Therese Winter,
from the *SPCK Book of Christian Prayer*

E

"THE EARTH HAS SKIN AND THAT SKIN HAS DISEASES; AND ONE OF ITS DISEASES IS CALLED MAN." F. NIETZSCHE.

F

Christmas Tree Recycling

2 Explain in your own words what stewardship is.

3 How significant do you think the activities in Source F are as examples of stewardship?

4 State and explain two contrasting examples of how Christians might demonstrate good stewardship of the environment.

ACTIVITY

In your class, brainstorm the rights and responsibilities that people have for their environment. Record them in a table like the one below. Can you think of any more rights? Try to think of at least one responsibility to go with each right.

Rights	Responsibilities
A beautiful world to live in	*Keep nature clean and tidy*
Food to eat	
Shelter	
Water to drink	
Clean air to breathe	

The response to environmental issues by Christian denominations

Christians tend to share similar views on the environment, whatever tradition they belong to, but there are differences in how individual Christians decide what action they are prepared to take.

G

1 The Earth and all life on it is a gift from God given to us to share and develop, not to dominate and exploit.

2 Our actions have consequences for the rights of others and for the resources of the Earth.

3 The goods of the Earth and the beauties of nature are to be enjoyed and celebrated as well as consumed.

4 We have the responsibility to create a balanced policy between consumption and conservation.

5 We must consider the welfare of future generations in our planning for and utilisation of the Earth's resources.

Pope John Paul in *Sollicitudo Rei Socialis*, 1988

I

The health of the environmental system is critical to all life and immensely fragile in the face of the demands of a consumerist and technologically powerful culture.

The universe as a whole is a product of God's creative and imaginative will. All its parts are interdependent. Men and women are to be stewards and curators, not exploiters, of its resources – material, animal and spiritual. Christians must support those working for conservation and the development of more appropriate, sustainable lifestyles.

Christian Faith Concerning the Environment, Methodist Conference, 1991

H

This Synod, affirming its belief and trust in God the Father who made the world, believes that the dominion given to human beings over the natural order is that of stewards who have to render an account, urges Her Majesty's Government:

a) to take all possible steps, both nationally and internationally, to establish a just and economical use of the Earth's energy resources, and to minimise the impact of consequential environmental pollution;

b) to take positive steps to curtail damage to flora and fauna by human activities in this country, and to seek to extend such restraint elsewhere in the world;

c) to consider what contribution it can make to the encouragement of the stabilising of the world's population so that human beings can live in sustainable harmony with the rest of the natural order and flourish without want;

and asks that dioceses be given the necessary information to consider what individual dioceses may do practically in the affirmation of this faith.

A motion agreed at the General Synod of the Church of England, 1992

FOCUS TASK

1 Use Sources G–I to draw up a table like this. In the first column write all the key Christian teachings on the environment. Tick the boxes when each teaching is included in the sources above.

Christian teaching on environment	Catholic	Anglican	Methodist

2 The problem with such statements from the Churches is that they are very general. Take one of the statements and:
   a) set three practical targets applying that statement
   b) plan how Christians in that tradition could celebrate meeting the targets
   c) decide what action they should take if they failed to meet the targets.

One Christian's response

Bonsall is on the edge of the Peak National Park and is designated as a conservation area by Derbyshire County Council. The main threats to its environment are from acid rain, transport and quarrying.

Ken Edgar is a father and grandfather who is committed to looking after the environment for future generations. He is an Anglican who was a church warden in the village church. He has served on the parish council since 1974.

Even the well-dressings have been affected by damage to the environment. We used to use black moss for the background but it is slow-growing, and in recent years it has been attacked by acid rain so now there is a preservation order on it and we have to use other natural materials.

The parish council tries to listen to people's concerns and act on them. At one time we were worried about the number of lorries parked on narrow roads in the village, so everyone in the village worked together to develop Church land into a lorry park with a children's play area by the side of it. This has been a great success.

I am worried, however, about the damage which is being done to the moors above the village. The rock contains valuable limestone and fluorspar. Firms are keen to extract it but do not meet their promises to reclaim the land afterwards. I think too many people are greedy and only worried about their own interests.

The parish church has little real power over environmental issues. We can comment on local planning applications if we think that the environment is in danger, but in the end we can't really stop anyone. To be honest, I don't feel my church has had much to say to me about the environment. Most of my sense of the fragility of the world comes from my science lessons at school.

ACTIVITY

1 Explain the beliefs that a Christian might have about the environment.
2 What threats are there to the environment in Bonsall? What can be done about them?
3 Do the Christians in Bonsall have more responsibility than the other villagers to look after the environment? Give more than one point of view to explain your answer.

1 'I am putting you in charge of the fish, the birds and all the wild animals.' (Genesis 1.28)
   Describe two different ways Christians might apply this verse to animal rights.
2 Do you think all Christians should be vegetarians? Explain your answer.

Animal rights versus human rights

Animal rights is another environmental dilemma. This is an issue on which Christian traditions vary. You are going to examine it by comparing the Catholic and Quaker teaching on this subject.

What is the relationship between human beings and animals?

Catholic theology does not accept that animals have rights. However, its teaching focuses on human duties towards animals. 'To deny animals rights is not to underestimate our obligation with regard to animal welfare. It is possible to oppose cruelty and exploitation without getting trapped into arguments about "rights". Animals, as our fellow creatures, should be a particular concern in our attitude towards creation.' 'We owe them kindness.' (from the Catholic Catechism).

Quaker:
The General Advice of 1926 says 'Let the law of kindness know no limits. Show a loving consideration for all God's creatures.' How Quakers apply this is up to them. Many would participate in the animal rights movement. Others would not.

Should Christians be vegetarians?

Certain uses of animals are acceptable to Catholics: they can be used to provide food and clothing. However, the use of animals for food requires consideration of potential suffering of the animal in slaughtering and transport.

Quakers were among the pioneer vegetarians of the 19th century. Today many Quakers are vegetarian, but it is a matter of choice. They have a larger proportion of vegetarians than other well-known denominations and at gatherings of young Quakers the diet is almost exclusively vegetarian.

What other uses of animals are acceptable or unacceptable?

Official teaching of the Catholic Church tolerates the use of animals in medical and scientific experiments 'if it remains within reasonable limits' and if this contributes to 'caring for or saving human lives'. Animals may be domesticated and used to help people in their work and leisure.

The most controversial area of animal welfare for Quakers is that of using animals for medical experiments. For over 100 years the Quaker Concern for Animals group has tried to influence other Quakers to resist vivisection on ethical grounds. But Quaker doctors and researchers who use animals in experiments justify this on the grounds of the gain to humans and animals in terms of knowledge.

Quakers have opposed hunting for 200 years and unite in condemning cruel exploitation for such trivial purposes as the testing of cosmetics and toiletries. Most Quakers would shun fur coats, circuses and zoos.

Human rights versus animal rights

The Catechism warns against exaggerated care being spent on animals, especially if money could be better spent on limiting human suffering. Catholics argue for a sense of balance. Animals are not human beings, they do not have rights, but they are owed respect and appropriate care.

Individual Quakers would apply their religious principles in different ways but they would try to balance the rights of humans with kindness to animals, to bring about the good of both.

Summarised from *What the Churches Say*, published by the Christian Education Movement

J

An anti-hunting demonstration in 1997

L

A service for Pet Sunday

FOCUS TASK

Write a paragraph in response to each of these questions.

1 How might a Christian decide whether to join the demonstration in Source J?
2 Explain what you think had happened in Source K and what the two protesters disagree about.
3 How might a Christian respond to the pet service in Source L?
4 How might a Christian respond to the speaker in Source M?
5 Devise an Animals' Charter for Christians to follow. Outline the rights and responsibilities of humans.

K

This mural protesting against the slaughter of cattle during the BSE crisis in 1996 was then itself defaced by protestors.

M

4.4 Is it ever right to fight?

A

In the Image of Man by Robert Henderson Blyth, painted just after the Second World War (1939–45)

Key questions for Christians

- How should Christians deal with conflicts?
- Is there ever a good reason to use violence?
- Should a Church ever support a war?
- How should Christians be working towards peace?

What do Christians believe about war?

Most Christians believe that war should be avoided. But many also believe that there are times when a Christian has to go to war. This is because they believe that the result of not going to war will be much worse.

The three main Christians stances towards war are shown in the diagram.

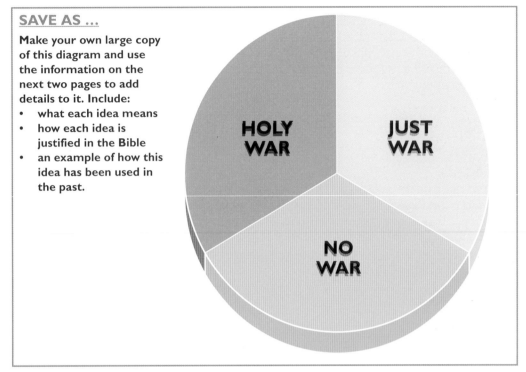

SAVE AS ...

Make your own large copy of this diagram and use the information on the next two pages to add details to it. Include:
- **what each idea means**
- **how each idea is justified in the Bible**
- **an example of how this idea has been used in the past.**

Holy war

Until the fourth century, Christian teaching was against the use of violence. Christians did not retaliate when persecuted, they did not join the army. However, all Christian teaching from this time about forgiveness, living at peace, not retaliating, is about the behaviour of individual Christians, not about national foreign policy.

As the Church became more politically powerful it faced a dilemma. The political leaders were Christians. Now they could affect the nation's foreign policy. Could the Church support a war?

There are examples in the Old Testament of God ordering war. For example, in 1 Samuel 15.2–3 God commands '[I will] punish the people of Amalek because their ancestors opposed the Israelites … Now go and attack the Amalekites and completely destroy everything they have.'

The idea developed of 'holy war' or war on behalf of God. The most famous examples of so-called holy war were the Christian wars to recover Jerusalem from the Muslims in the Middle Ages. Christians called them the Crusades, Muslims called them the Frankish invasions.

Whether the Church leaders who started the Crusades actually believed they were a holy war or just used that idea to win the support of the majority of ordinary Christians is not clear. Many of those fighting were certainly convinced that they were fighting a holy war on God's behalf.

The Crusades were a disaster. They soured relations between Western Europe and the Middle East to this day. They did not achieve any military objective. Terrible atrocities were committed in the name of God. Whole cities of people were slaughtered.

B

Jerusalem is the navel of the world. This royal city is now held captive by her enemies and is enslaved by a people which does not acknowledge God. She asks you to rescue her. All men going there who die, whether on the journey or while fighting the pagans will immediately be forgiven their sins. Until now you have fought and killed one another. Stop these hatreds amongst yourselves, silence the quarrels. Instead, rescue the Holy Land from that dreadful race.

Pope Urban's recruiting speech in 1095

I Read Source B. How Christian do you think it is to say such things?

Just war

In the 13th century Thomas Aquinas, a Christian monk and one of the most influential theologians of the last 1,000 years, drew up some conditions for a just war, based on ideas of Augustine in the fourth century. How could the Church help the leaders of a state to decide whether a war was just?

C

Aquinas laid down three conditions:

1. *The war must be started and controlled by the authority of the state or ruler.*
2. *There must be a just cause; those attacked must deserve it.*
3. *The war must be fought to promote good or avoid evil. Peace and justice must be restored afterwards.*

The test of a just war was a useful one. Further conditions were later added by other Christians:

4. *The war must be the last resort; all other possible ways of solving the problem have been tried.*
5. *There must be 'proportionality' in the way the war is fought, e.g. innocent civilians should not be killed. Only enough force should be used as is needed to achieve victory.*
6. *The good gained by the victory must be greater than the evil which led to the war.*

I **Do you think that the fight against Hitler's Germany in the Second World War met all six conditions for a just war in Source C? You can get a sheet from your teacher to help you.**

The two World Wars

The First World War, also called the Great War, changed people's perception of the idea of a just war. Many people entered this war believing it to be just. But by the end many were convinced that it failed most of the tests. However, the idea reoccurred in the fight against Hitler in the Second World War.

Wars of defence

Many Christians still believe in the possibility of a just war and would be prepared to join an army if they felt that they were fighting against evil. The Church of England for example accepts that the government has a duty to defend the nation, and that therefore a war may, at times, be just and right. Some Christians agree that war may be 'the lesser of two evils'. It may indeed be a way of 'loving your neighbour' to go to war to defend another country. The Commandment 'Do not kill' is not used in the Bible to apply to killing in a war.

D

I believe the armed forces are an extension of the police force. They're seeking to maintain law and order, but on an international level. It is important to have Christians involved in law and order. Our God is a God of justice, and Christians need to help maintain justice in the world. I think that a valid way of doing this is through working in the army.

The Revd A Carter, a Christian army chaplain

Civil war

Wars between countries are actually less common in the modern world than wars within countries (civil wars). Few of the just war criteria can be applied to civil wars, sometimes differing religious beliefs can actually cause civil war. Civil wars are also infamous for their devastating effects on civilians. Civil war is one of the main causes of poverty, starvation and refugee problems in the world today.

E

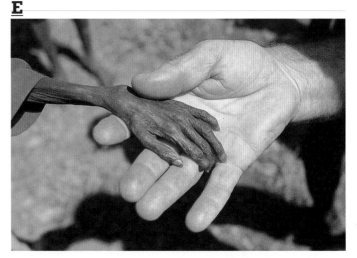

This photograph, taken in Uganda in 1980, shows a Catholic priest holding the hand of a starving Ugandan child during a famine caused by civil war.

F

We utterly deny all outward wars and strife, and fightings with outward weapons, for any end, or under any pretence whatever.

The Quakers announced their rejection of the idea of a just war in 1660, when Britain had just emerged from a bitter Civil War in which many Quakers had been involved

H

Look at how much of his own moral code man has to break in war. He defeats his own ends. Evil can only be overcome by good. We have enough evidence from history to show that the overthrow of violence by violence produces more violence.

The Methodist minister, Lord Soper, a celebrated 20th-century pacifist

No war

A pacifist is someone who believes that all war is wrong and who would refuse to participate in any fighting. Among Christian denominations, the Quakers are the group most associated with pacifism.

Conscientious objectors
During the First World War Quakers founded the No-Conscription Fellowship, which supported people who refused to join the army on religious or ethical grounds.

G

The life, teaching and death of my Lord, Jesus Christ, opposes in every sense the method of life which leads to strife among men. I am doing my best by God's help to live in that way of life which takes away the occasion of all wars.

Owing to the present attitude of the Wesleyan Church on the war question [they supported it] I have after long consideration resigned my connection with it. I am now attending the Ealing meeting of the Society of Friends [Quakers].

Alexander Sim, writing to a military tribunal in 1916, asking to be excused military service as a conscientious objector

There is plenty in the Bible to support pacifism. 'Do not kill' is one of the Ten Commandments, although in the Old Testament this did not include killing in war. Jesus spoke a great deal about peace, for example, 'Blessed are the peacemakers', 'Love your enemies and pray for those who persecute you', 'Be perfect, therefore, as your heavenly Father is perfect.' (Matthew 5.9, 44, 48)

When Jesus was arrested one of his followers took out his sword and attacked one of the men who had come to arrest Jesus, cutting off his right ear. 'But Jesus said, "Enough of this!" He touched the man's ear and healed him.' (Luke 22.49–51) In another version of the same story, in Matthew 26.52, Jesus says: 'All who take the sword will die by the sword.' He told his followers that when they were struck they were not to strike back but to turn the other cheek. He rejected the idea of revenge. He put those things in the hands of God.

Pacifism in the nuclear age
Since the Second World War most governments have assumed that the best way to avoid a war is to be strong enough to win one should it happen. This argument was behind the colossal build-up of armaments in the arms race of the 1970s and 1980s. Eventually the superpowers had enough weapons to destroy each other 80 times over. Supporters of this approach point out that these weapons have kept peace in Europe for a longer period than ever before.

On the other hand, the threat of nuclear war drove many people into pacifism. Christians were at the forefront of the nuclear disarmament campaign. For example, at the Faslane Peace Camp Scottish Christians called for Britain to abolish its Trident and Polaris nuclear missiles.

Some Christians oppose nuclear war, but believe that conventional weapons are needed in the modern world. They call themselves 'nuclear pacifists'.

Christian pacifists argue that war:

- is a waste of resources given by God
- is a cause of immense suffering, including the suffering of innocent people
- encourages and exaggarates the baser and undesirable human instincts – greed, hatred, prejudice.

These effects will always outweigh any argument that war is just.

FOCUS TASK

1. **Does the fact that Britain has a strong army and its own nuclear weapons make you feel safe or scared? Explain why.**
2. **The government has declared war. Explain how a Christian would decide whether or not to join the armed forces.**
3. **Peace is not just 'absence of war'. Complete the sentence 'Peace is …' as many times as you can. Share your ideas with the rest of the class and choose the five statements which best express the Christian idea of peace.**
4. **'Christians should always forgive and never retaliate. War is always wrong for a Christian.'**

   Write an essay discussing this statement, showing that you have thought about both sides of the debate.

The arms trade

Britain's 'security' has a price. Defence, at 8 per cent, is the second biggest category of government expenditure (see Source J). Arms manufacture is also one of Britain's most successful industries. It provides jobs for more than half a million people. Arms exports amount to billions of pounds per year.

J

Money spent in 1995 by the British Government
Health – £40.8 billion
Defence – £23.2 billion
Education – £14.4 billion
Overseas aid – £3.2 billion

ACTIVITY A

Imagine you are the administrator of a large British cathedral, which has spent millions of pounds on renovations, so you need as much money as you can raise. One money-raising venture is a series of high-profile concerts to celebrate the 300th anniversary of the cathedral, with local businesses invited to sponsor each event.

An offer is made by an arms manufacturer. The company, which makes Stealth bombers (which can slip through radar detectors) and Trident (nuclear missile-launching submarines) among other things, offers you sponsorship of £15,000 in return for their name on the programme and a row of seats at the concerts for their guests.

What do you decide? And why?

I

The Tower of Babel, an engraving by Japanese Christian artist Takako Horino

Activity A describes a real situation faced by St Paul's Cathedral in London. They accepted the deal. This was their justification:

- The company makes other things as well as armaments.
- They do not sell to irresponsible governments.
- They are not underhand about their arms sales. They avoid corrupt practice.
- They said they wanted to feed something back into the local community.

However, other Christians did not agree:

K

1 Imagine you are a Christian working in an arms factory. How would you respond to Source K?

The Church should be taking a lead on this issue. This decision lends approval to the arms trade. It seems to us that the Church has rewritten the sixth Commandment: 'Thou shalt not kill … unless you make a whacking great profit out of it.'

Rachel Harford of the Campaign Against Arms Trade

L

I thought that the Somoza government was so unjust that I had to join the resistance movement. As a Christian it was the only conclusion I could reach, but when I did so my Church could not understand why I was willing to fight and they expelled me.

Pablo read in the Bible that Jesus offered a just and fair life for all people. Most Nicaraguans did not have such a life so he decided to become an armed revolutionary.

Violence v. non-violence in the struggle for liberation

As you saw on pages 62–3, many Christians have found themselves involved in struggles against injustice in their own country. Is taking up arms an acceptable option in these circumstances? Some Christians think so, as you can see from Sources L–N.

Other Christians would argue that the only way to improve a bad situation is through non-violent action: marches, sit-ins, letters or demonstrations such as Source O. They believe that non-violent action is morally superior to violence because it is voluntary, dignifying and creative.

M

Jesus as a liberation fighter with a gun

N

One day it happened that a group of boys and girls from Solentiname, because of profound convictions and after having let it mature for a long time, decided to take up arms. Why did they do it? They did it for only one reason: their love for the kingdom of God, for the ardent desire that a just society be implanted, a real and concrete kingdom of God on Earth. When the time came, these boys and girls fought with great courage, but they also fought as Christians. That morning at San Carlos they tried several times with a loudspeaker to reason with the guardsmen so they might not have to fire a single shot. But the guardsmen responded to their reasoning with sub-machine-gun fire. With great regret they also were forced to shoot. Alejandro, one from my community, entered the building when in it there were no longer any but dead or wounded soldiers. He was going to set fire to it but, out of consideration for the wounded, he did not do it. I congratulate myself that these young Christians fought without hate – above all without hate for the wounded guardsmen, poor peasants like themselves, also exploited.

From a letter to the people of Nicaragua by the Catholic priest Ernesto Cardenal in December 1977. He was banned by his Church for supporting the revolutionaries, but after the success of the Revolution became a minister for education in the new government.

O

A peace vigil in Derry, Northern Ireland, in August 1995, to mark the first anniversary of the terrorist groups' ceasefire

ACTIVITY B

Imagine that Ernesto Cardenal (Source N) meets one of the people taking part in the peace vigil in Source O. What might they say to each other about Christian attitudes to violence?

FOCUS TASK

1 Describe in your own words what is meant by the terms 'holy war' and 'just war'.

2 Choose one 20th-century war and explain whether you think it was a 'holy war', a 'just war' or neither. Give reasons to support your opinion.

3 Explain why some religious believers take part in war and others refuse to do so.

Global issues – Review task

1 Describe in your own words the message of this cartoon.
2 Explain three Christian beliefs about Creation which might affect Christians' attitudes towards this cartoon.
3 Choose one global issue which you have studied and explain:
   a) why it is a problem which worries Christians and why it needs an urgent response
   b) what different viewpoints Christians might take towards this issue
   c) whether Christians have more duty than other people to take action on this issue.

UNIT 5

Arguments about God

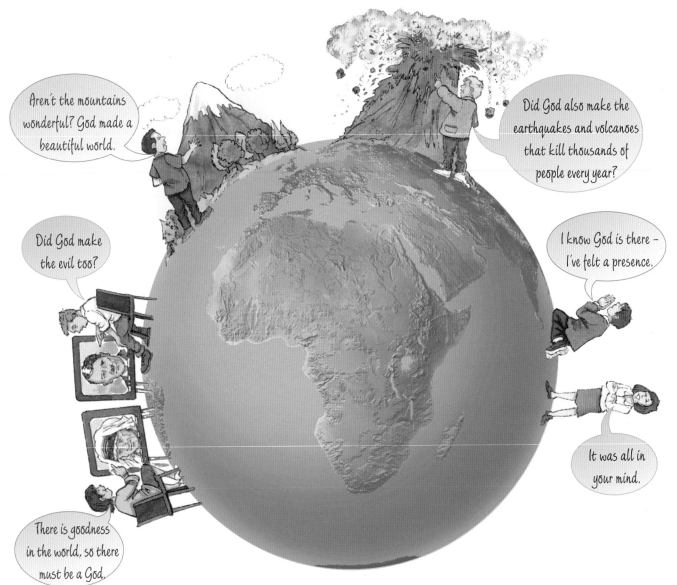

This unit takes a different approach from Units 2–4. Rather than looking at moral dilemmas and issues you will be studying arguments about God and religion.

Arguing is a natural part of everyday life. It is also the best way to clarify ideas. Someone has an idea. Someone else disagrees with it. They argue. One persuades the other, or not, depending on how convincing their arguments are. This is how philosophers work.

It is also how this unit works. Start by studying the arguments in the cartoon and, with a partner, role play one of the arguments. Before you start you should note down some of the main points that your character might use in their argument.

5.1 Why do people believe in God?

✓ CHECKPOINT

You will need to be sure you can use these terms: ATHEIST (someone who does not believe there is a God), THEIST (someone who does believe a God exists) and AGNOSTIC (someone who says we cannot know whether a God exists).

A

In my life there have been many occasions when circumstances have changed for good as a result of prayer. Some people call it coincidence; I call it God.

B

As an atheist, I cannot accept there is a God. It makes no sense. I have never felt that a God exists. There is just this life here and now and it's up to us to make the most of our opportunities while we are alive.

C

I think there is a God, but he's short-staffed. He's starting a project on another planet and he's left his brother-in-law in charge here.

Jasper Carrott, comedian

D

I firmly believe in the existence of God. I believe God is present in all our lives as a positive force for good. How else can you explain the way that people try to be good and caring towards other humans?

Does God exist?

E

If there is a God, why is there death? Why is there so much suffering in the world?

ACTIVITY

1 Make your own copy of this belief line.
2 Decide where you think each of Sources A–G should be placed on the line. Mark the spot with the appropriate letter.
3 Mark the spot on the line where you think your own beliefs about God would appear. Record the reason for your decision.
4 Now ask two other people in your class what they think about God. Record their explanations and mark their views on the belief line.

SAVE AS …

5 Write your own definitions of the words 'atheist', 'theist' and 'agnostic', using examples from Sources A–G.

I believe in God
— 5
— 4
— 3
— 2
— 1
— 0   I'm not sure
— 1
— 2
— 3
— 4
— 5
I don't believe in God

F

I cannot be certain that God exists, but I'm not prepared to say God definitely does not exist. I guess you would call me an agnostic. I think religious questions are really important but impossible to answer! What do you mean, anyway, when you use the word 'God'?

G

I would never be without the idea that there is some hidden force that was responsible for the Creation. I wouldn't be satisfied with just being a humanist and thinking that it's just me and my brain and my thoughts.

Kim Wallinger, lead singer of rock band World Party

Reasons to believe

Maybe it was quite easy to place yourself on the belief line, but you may have found it much more difficult to explain *why* you placed yourself where you did. Most people find it very difficult to explain their beliefs. One aim of this book is to help you to do this.

When people give reasons for their beliefs certain ideas appear again and again. The most common ones are summarised in the table below.

Why people believe in God	Examples	Why people do not believe in God	Examples
• Science shows beauty and order in the natural world, which must have been created by somebody		• Because of suffering, chaos and evil in the world	
• Because they have 'experienced' God for themselves		• Because God is silent	
• Because their parents or community have brought them up to believe in God		• Because they dislike believers they have met	
• Because they are afraid of what might happen to them if they do not believe		• Because science has disproved religion	

H

Let us weigh the gain and the loss, in wagering that God exists. Consider these alternatives: if you win, you win all; if you lose you lose nothing. Do not hesitate therefore to wager that God exists.

Blaise Pascal, French philosopher and mathematician, 1623–62

I

No rain, no mushrooms!
No God, no world!

African proverb

J

As a child, nothing put me off God more than my schoolteachers' highly selective habit of claiming to see him in whatever suited them – be it a daffodil or the abundance of nature. He was there, they said, in the stars. You could even tell he existed by watching the television programmes of David Attenborough!

But taking everything which is good or beautiful as evidence of God always struck me as a particularly dishonest habit … When you think about it, it is an astonishingly feeble gambit. It can all too easily be countered by equally impressive arguments: 'When I look at a small child, buried at three with cancer, or when I contemplate that famous first charge in the Battle of the Somme [First World War], then I know that he doesn't.'

David Hare, playwright and agnostic, speaking to Anglican clergy in Westminster Abbey, 1996

K

God is the refuge of the incompetent, the helpless, the miserable. They find not only sanctuary in his arms but also a kind of superiority, soothing to their macerated egos. He will set them above their betters.

H.L. Mencken, American writer and atheist, 1956

FOCUS TASK

Make your own copy of the table above. Record examples of people using this argument for or against believing in God. Start by recording examples from Sources A–K. Add more arguments if you need to.

Keep the table and add to it throughout this unit.

5.2 Can you prove that God exists?

As you saw on page 91, there are many reasons for Christians to believe that God exists. People also have many reasons to believe there is no God. You are going to look at some of the reasons in greater detail and see how well they stand up when challenged. You will look at three different arguments.

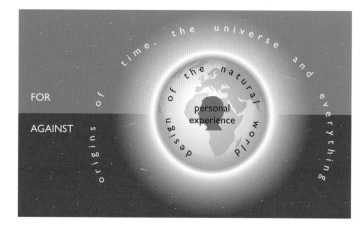

Key questions for Christians

- Where did the universe come from?
- Did life on Earth happen by design or by chance?
- Is religious experience real or illusory?

Argument 1: Origins of the universe

A common argument for believing in God is that the universe must have come from somewhere. Christians believe it came from God.

An early version of this belief is the Creation story in the Bible. In Chapters 1 and 2 of Genesis God creates the universe and everything in it (see page 96).

Philosophers have used the existence of the universe as an argument for the existence of God.

Aquinas and the First Cause

Thomas Aquinas was one of the leading scholars of the Middle Ages. Seven hundred years ago he devised several arguments for the existence of God. One of his arguments was the 'First Cause' argument (see Source A).

The Big Bang

Recent discoveries in science have given the First Cause argument new life.

The theory of the Big Bang is that once, all matter in the universe was concentrated into an incredibly dense mass. It was much smaller than the eye of a needle. For some reason, 15,000 million years ago it began to expand.

This expansion is called 'The Big Bang' although this term was originally used by the theory's critics to ridicule it! A better image might be 'The Big Bloom', as the opening out of the universe was orderly, like a flower blooming, although with the speed and force of an explosion.

From that point, the universe has continued its rapid expansion to this day, and our Earth, like all the planets, stars and matter in the universe, comes from the cooling and gathering of matter sent out by the big bang. The universe will one day stop expanding and start contracting.

One alternative theory – the Steady State theory – says that the universe is not changing and had no beginning, and that therefore the Big Bang is nonsense. However, few scientists today accept the Steady State theory.

Where else could the universe come from?

A

Everything in the universe has a cause. Trace those causes back and there must have been a First Cause that triggered everything else. God is that First Cause.

Thomas Aquinas' First Cause argument

What caused the Big Bang?

The Big Bang theory is widely accepted by people today – including many Christians – even though there are unanswered and currently unanswerable questions about it. You can probably see the attraction of the theory to some Christians. From the religious point of view the most important unanswered question is what triggered the Big Bang.

Chance?

Some say it was pure chance; that in the particular unusual conditions that prevailed 15,000 million years ago, what we now recognise as the laws of cause and effect did not apply. No one was needed to cause the expansion of the universe. This is an explanation favoured by atheists and agnostics.

God?

An alternative view is that it was an act of God that in some way triggered the Big Bang. This position is favoured by theists. In Aquinas' terms, God was the First Cause which triggered the Big Bang.

B

Most people believe that God allows the universe to evolve according to a set of laws and does not intervene to break those laws ... but it would still be up to God to wind up the clockwork and choose how to start it off. So long as the universe had a beginning, we could suppose it had a Creator.

From *A Brief History of Time* by Professor Stephen Hawking, 1988

C

For the scientist who has lived by his faith in the power of reason, the story ends like a bad dream. He has scaled the mountains of ignorance; he is about to conquer the highest peak; and as he pulls himself over the final rock, he is greeted by a band of theologians who have been sitting there for centuries!

Robert Jastrow, American Christian astrophysicist

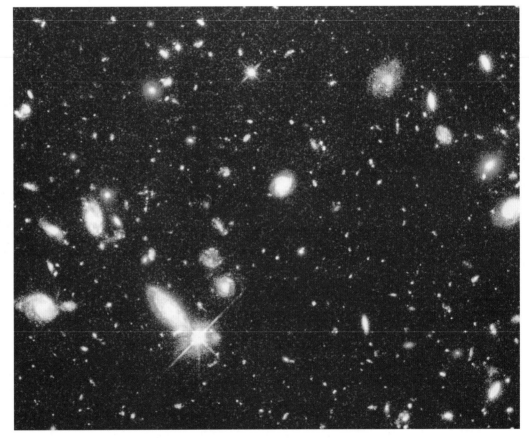

FOCUS TASK

1   Write your own 'postcard-sized' summaries of:
    a)   **The First Cause argument**
    b)   **The Big Bang theory.**
2   **What point is being made in Source C?**
3   **Which explanation of the Big Bang do you favour:**
    a)   **that it was caused by chance, or**
    b)   **that it was caused by God, or**
    c)   **that it never happened?**
    Explain your view, showing that you have considered an alternative viewpoint.

Argument 2: The design of the natural world

> Such an intricate world must have been designed by someone.

D

A second common argument Christians give for God's existence is that the world around them shows a pattern and therefore it must have been created or designed by someone. This is known as the argument of 'design' – the belief that everything in the human body and the natural world is so intricately designed that this could not have happened by random chance.

> This is my quiet and peaceful time of day when I watch the foxes in the garden . . . and reflect on the day. I believe very strongly in God – my upbringing was built on that foundation. And every time I look into the garden I'm convinced. Who else could make the trees?
>
> Mr Motivator, television fitness-trainer

Two famous Christians in history based their 'design' arguments around a thumb and a watch.

ACTIVITY A

Choose Source E or F and, before reading the material that follows, see if you can think how someone might use it to argue that God exists.

E

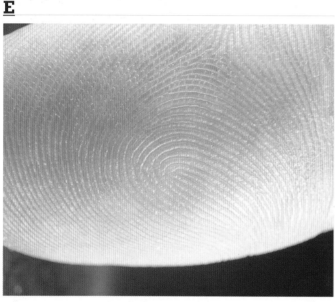

F

Newton and the thumb

Sir Isaac Newton, 1642–1727, one of the founders of modern science, said: 'In the absence of any other proof, the thumb alone would convince me of God's existence.' Newton believed that such intricate designs as the human thumb, unique to each individual, must have had a designer.

SAVE AS ...

Make sure you have recorded the arguments of both Newton and Paley on your copy of the table on page 91, using their examples or your own.

Paley and the watch

One hundred years after Newton, William Paley (1743–1805), a philosopher, used a watch to explain why he believed in God. Paley's argument was more complicated than Newton's. He compared the watch to the world. In the 18th century a watch was one of the most intricate pieces of machinery made by human beings.

Paley argued that if he were to find a watch lying on the ground, he would assume that it was the product of a designer for, unlike a stone, he would see at once that it was made up of many different parts which worked together to produce movement. If any one of these parts was ordered slightly differently then the whole structure would not work. Paley argued that, in the same way, the world is like a machine, and if the world is like a machine, it must have a designer. Paley concluded that this designer is God.

Nietzsche and an imperfect world

There are problems with both Newton's and Paley's arguments. The 19th-century German philosopher Friedrich Nietzsche completely disagreed with them. He argued that God was 'dead'!

Nietzsche refused to see order in the world. Take, for example, the way the Earth's crust is made up of plates which do not fit together precisely. This causes tremors, volcanoes and earthquakes. 'How could a God who is good create a world so imperfect?' argued Nietzsche.

Nietzsche concluded that there was no God, there were no natural laws, and there was no order. Scientists had made incorrect observations about the world and had invented laws based on these. Nietzsche believed that there is no absolute truth about the world and no ultimate purpose, a view known as 'nihilism'.

Epicurus and the problem of evil

Others have gone further and said that there are not merely faults in the world; there is evil and therefore there cannot be a God. The Greek philosopher Epicurus (342–270 BCE) described a very neat argument against God based on this belief (see the diagram below). You will return to the problem of evil on pages 114–20.

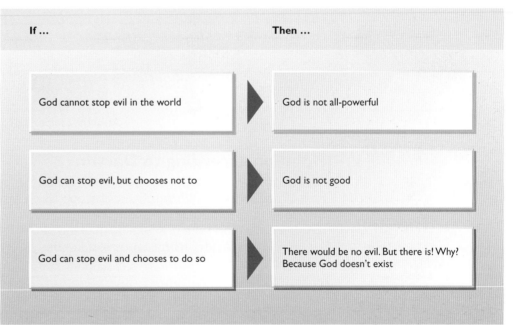

If ...	Then ...
God cannot stop evil in the world	God is not all-powerful
God can stop evil, but chooses not to	God is not good
God can stop evil and chooses to do so	There would be no evil. But there is! Why? Because God doesn't exist

ACTIVITY B

Ancient Greek philosophers such as Epicurus would discuss problems like the existence of God in the street or over drinks.

In an imaginary café (which does not exist in regular time) Paley meets Nietzsche, Epicurus, or Darwin. What do you think they might say to each other over coffee?

Darwin and natural selection

A scientific challenge to the design argument came from the theory of evolution (see page 96). In the 19th century Charles Darwin (1809–82) developed his theory that all life evolves by natural selection. The animals or plants that are best suited to their environment survive. Those that are not die out. According to this theory, human, animal and plant life had designed itself!

FOCUS TASK

'If God designed the world, I think that he should be sacked.'

1 Explain in your own words what the speaker means.
2 Explain whether you agree or disagree with this statement. Support your answer with reference to material from pages 94 and 95. Show that you have considered another viewpoint.

Interlude: how do Christians interpret Genesis 1 and 2?

Let's briefly step aside from exploring arguments for the existence of God and look in more detail at the relationship of religion and science, and specifically the apparent conflict between creation and evolution.

To many Christians the Big Bang and evolution seem plausible explanations for the origins of the universe and of life on Earth. Yet they differ in many details from the creation stories in Genesis 1 and 2.

How does this affect the way Christians read the Creation stories at the beginning of the Bible?

G

An artist's impression of Creation according to the Bible

Evolution according to Darwin

In past centuries many people believed the Bible's account of Creation to be literally true. In the 17th century Archbishop Ussher even calculated the exact time when God finally finished Creation (9 a.m. on Friday 23 October, 4004 BCE).

With the development of scientific thinking in the 19th century, and particularly the theory of evolution, many aspects of the Bible Creation story were questioned (see Source H).

H

1 **Give two examples of the way that the theory of evolution challenged the story given in Genesis 1 and 2.**
2 **The Bible describes in Genesis 2.7 how God 'breathed into man', and in Genesis 1.26 how God created man 'in his image'. Discuss what you think this means.**
3 **Do you think these beliefs can be held alongside the concept of evolution? Give reasons for your answer.**
4 **How might Genesis 1 and 2 give meaning, value or purpose to a Christian's life?**

Time scale
The process science was describing took many hundreds of millions of years. The process according to the Bible took six days.

Process
Darwin's 'natural selection' was an unguided process. There were no rights and wrongs, just the strong and the weak – the world had designed itself through the survival of the fittest. The Bible had God very firmly in charge.

The place of human life
Evolution had human beings evolving from apes. The Bible had humans made 'in God's image' on the sixth day of Creation.

5 Source K suggests that Genesis 1 and 2 conveys powerful ideas about God. Look back at pages 14, 36 and 76 in this book. For each issue, find out how Christians could apply Genesis 1 and 2. What 'powerful ideas about God' does it contain?

6 Do you think it would affect a Christian's attitudes to these issues if they did not believe in a literal interpretation of the Bible?

What kind of truth is Genesis 1 and 2?

Some Christians found Darwin's theory a threat to their faith, because it appeared to challenge the authority of the Bible. If the Bible was wrong on this, might it be wrong on other things too? They preferred to maintain a 'literalist' reading of Genesis 1 and 2 (see Source I). This viewpoint is known as Creationism. Creationists have succeeded in banning the teaching of the theory of evolution in some states in the USA.

However, other Christians see no contradiction between Genesis 1 and 2 and scientific theories such as evolution. They see no conflict generally between science and religion. Many scientists are Christian believers, as was Darwin.

When they consider the Bible, these Christians do not look for scientific truth. What they expect the Bible to give them is the truth about God and God's relationship with human beings. They see natural selection as a plausible, if unproved, explanation for life on Earth. They see Genesis 1 and 2 as an authoritative account of God's relationship with human beings and other living creatures.

I

I don't believe evolution is true. I believe Creation is true: that God created the world in six, 24-hour days. If there is a God, he can do anything. If God created by evolution, it doesn't give him half the glory it would if he created the world from scratch. Scientific knowledge is human knowledge. I prefer to trust God's truth because he has been there from the beginning.

Astrid, a London student, explains why she wears this tee-shirt saying 'Our Father?! Evolution: the wisdom of men is foolishness to God (1 Corinthians 1.20)'.

J

Science asks how things have happened, religion asks why. Genesis is not there to give short, technical answers about how the universe began. It gives us the big answer that things exist because of God's will. One can perfectly well believe in the Big Bang, but believe in it as well as the will of God the creator.

John Polkinghorne, a Christian and a scientist at Cambridge University

K

The Bible contains many different kinds of literature: poems, proverbs, history, letters, allegories, parables, etc. The first task in reading the creation stories is to decide what kind of writing this is. Genesis 1 and 2 bears all the marks of being a poem, or a hymn, or a teaching to be used in worship. Such poetry has the strength of conveying powerful ideas about God, but all the limitations in scientific understanding that you would expect of a writer of many thousands of years ago limited to their own scientific knowledge.

Dr David Wilkinson, an astrophysicist

FOCUS TASK

1 Create a design for a tee-shirt that sums up what *you* believe about the origins of life.

2 Explain how far different Christians would agree with your ideas. Refer to the sources on this page in your answer.

> I know God exists.
> Who else healed me?

Argument 3: Religious experience

A third argument for the existence of God is religious experience. People meet God. They feel God. They hear God. Or they say they do! For them, their experience is the ultimate proof. But is it enough to convince others?

Was John Rajah healed by God?

In 1987 John Rajah, an insurance worker, developed stomach pains. In the summer of 1988 his condition rapidly worsened.

> I was in hospital for weeks. I had blood poisoning. I wasn't able to eat or drink. I was fed into my neck through my veins. I lost the vision in my left eye and a disc disintegrated in my spine. I was very close to death and I cried out to God. I was only 24 years old and I didn't want to die.
>
> I had a vision of two tunnels – a dark tunnel on the left and a dark tunnel on the right with a light at the end of it. I instinctively knew I had to make a choice. I put my foot into the tunnel with light and hoped for life.
>
> After that experience I decided to seek God.

> The doctors did not know what caused John's disease, a form of colitis. Surgery was a last resort. His colon was removed. He had a colostomy bag instead. He wore a surgical corset, to support his spine. He was in constant pain and walked hunched over like an old man.
>
> In summer 1990 John came to Holy Trinity, Brompton, an Evangelical Anglican church. At the end of the service, the vicar invited people to come forward for prayer. John felt at peace and went forward. He made a commitment to follow Jesus.

1 **Explain the role of each of the following in John Rajah's healing:**
- **a vision**
- **prayer**
- **other Christians**
- **John's own actions**
- **miraculous intervention by God.**

> I followed up my commitment to God by joining an 'Alpha course' at my church (an Alpha Course is an introduction to Christianity, commonly used in evangelical churches). On 18 March 1992 the talk was on healing and the team began to pray for the sick. Two people said they felt there was someone present with problems regarding their colon and God wanted to heal them. The leader asked that if anyone was present with the disease colitis they come forward for prayer. I thought, 'This has got to be me!' They prayed for me.
>
> At the time I did not feel any different. But I went home and decided I was going to have faith that God had healed me. I decided to put aside all my medication and, trusting completely in God's word, prayed in hope.
>
> When I woke up the next day there was no pain and I wasn't bleeding! I was unsure of what was going on and for a while I was scared but realised God had touched me. From that day on, I became fitter and stronger and no longer depended on tablets. It was amazing – Jesus healed me and set me free.
>
> The effects of surgery and its consequences from the years of illness are still present but I am not daunted because God has healed me, is still healing me and will continue to heal me.

I am John's sister. I am a doctor. At the time of John's medical problems I was not a Christian, but through seeing him miraculously get better and hearing his account of his cure, I came to believe in the possibility that God had healed him. I went on an Alpha course to find out more and, through John's healing, I too am now a Christian.

Dr Christine Rajah

✓ CHECKPOINT

Other forms of experience
John Rajah's is only one sort of experience. On pages 108–13 you will study many other forms of religious experience. You will need to think about whether such experiences are more or less convincing evidence of the existence of God than the story of John Rajah.

When people read a story like John Rajah's, they tend to find evidence to support their existing ideas. If they do believe that God can heal someone in this way then they find evidence to support their belief. If not, then they find evidence to confirm their doubt.

The believer might say that the doubter's spiritual awareness is underdeveloped so they cannot see God at work. The sceptic will say that the believer's spiritual awareness is overdeveloped so they see God in things that have a rational explanation.

FOCUS TASK A

1 Work in pairs and take one role each – a believer and a doubter. The believer should argue that John Rajah's experience proves the existence of God, the doubter should argue that his experience has other explanations.
2 Swap roles and repeat the exercise.
3 In your own words, explain the difficulties facing someone:
   a) trying to disprove someone else's experience of God
   b) trying to prove their own experience of God.
4 'Religious experience is illusion rather than reality.'
   Write three paragraphs to explain how far you agree or disagree with this statement. In your answer show that you have considered other points of view. Illustrate your answer from the experience of John Rajah or from other religious experiences you have studied.

FOCUS TASK B

Work in groups.

1 Make a large simplified copy of the diagram from page 92 on an A3 piece of paper.
2 Write each of the statements on the right on a separate slip of paper.
3 Place each statement where you think it best fits on your diagram. Try to agree the positions with the rest of the group.
4 Once you have agreed all the positions, paste the statements onto the diagram.
5 You are now ready to write up your findings in an essay about arguments for and against the existence of God. Write a paragraph on each argument, making sure you have summarised both why some people accept it and why other people reject it. Conclude with your own view as to whether God exists, explaining why you believe this but showing that you have considered other points of view.

Religious experience is all in the mind.

There is God-given order in the natural world.

God has answered my prayers.

God is the First Cause of the universe.

There is cruelty and suffering in the natural world.

The Big Bang happened by chance.

5.3   What is God like?

Images of God

Most people have an image of God, even if it is simply an image of something they do not believe in!

A class of students in a Christian school in England were asked to draw their ideas about God. Sources A–D show some of their drawings.

A

B

ACTIVITY

1   Look carefully at Sources **A–D.**
2   Choose the idea that is nearest to your own image of God. Write down three reasons why you chose it. If none of them is near, go straight to Question 3.
3   Choose the idea that is furthest away from your image of God. Write down three reasons why you chose that one.
4   Do you think the people who drew Sources **A–D** believe this is what **God** actually looks like? Explain your answer.
5   Many religions forbid drawings or images of God. The second of the Ten Commandments forbids it. Why do you think this is? Exodus 20.4 may help you.

C

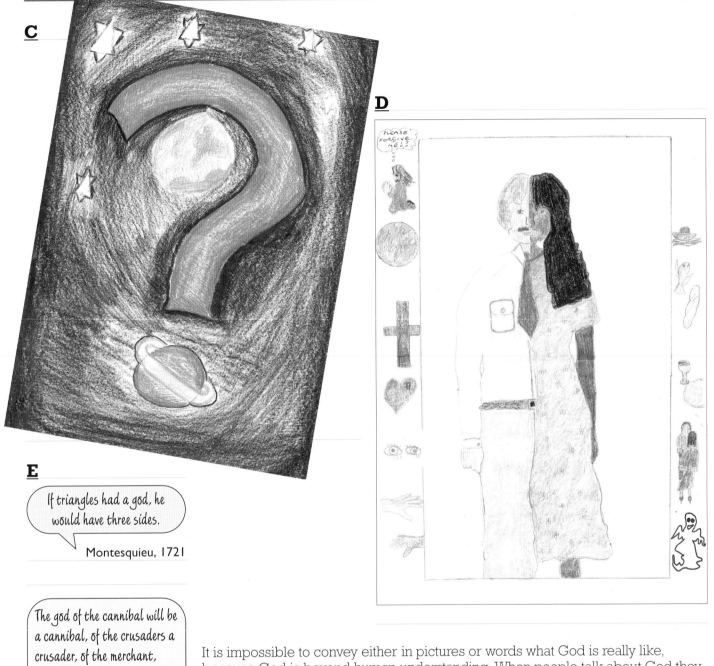

D

E

> If triangles had a god, he would have three sides.
>
> Montesquieu, 1721

> The god of the cannibal will be a cannibal, of the crusaders a crusader, of the merchant, a merchant.
>
> Emerson, 1860

> God is what man finds that is divine in himself. God is the best way man can behave in the ordinary occasions of life and the farthest point to which man can stretch himself.
>
> Max Lerner, 1959

It is impossible to convey either in pictures or words what God is really like, because God is beyond human understanding. When people talk about God they therefore use pictures or concrete images or symbolic language to convey some selected quality of God. They sometimes use human images – e.g. calling God a shepherd or a king – this is known as 'ANTHROPOMORPHISM'. These human images help others to picture God, but at the same time they limit God. It might seem that God is simply a bigger, better human being. This is the criticism expressed by the speakers in Source E.

You will need to keep this idea in mind over the next six pages as you examine various Christian ideas about God. Thinking and writing about God is interesting, but also open to misunderstanding, so it requires a lot of patience!

I   How might a Christian respond to the statements in Source E?

Key questions for Christians

- Is it possible to describe God at all?
- Why do people's images of God vary so much?
- Do Christians believe in one God or three?
- Was Jesus God or man or both?

Personal or impersonal?

Some Christians feel that God is impersonal, unknowable and mysterious; others that God is personal and close.

Both ideas can be found in the Bible itself. Sometimes God is described almost as a friend to human beings, directly concerned with the feelings and needs of people. At other times God is presented as a dangerous force: catch a glimpse and something terrible will happen to you.

Personal – Many Christians believe that individuals can have a relationship with God. This has led them to talk as if God were a person with human emotions and characteristics, to whom they can feel close and who supports and cares for individuals in their everyday lives. The evangelical tradition particularly emphasises these personal qualities of God. Whether and how a Christian prays is a good test of their image of God, because prayer is supposed to be a direct communication between a Christian and God. The prayers of someone who believes in a personal God will be almost like a conversation with a friend. Others see a personal God as a ruler who is more powerful than them and commands respect.

Such ideas, whilst allowing Christians to relate to God, are also limiting. Plainly, God can not be a person. A person cannot be present everywhere at once, answering all prayers and meeting all needs. God is eternal, so cannot be young or old. To be 'a friend' to everyone, God needs to be much more than a person.

Others talk of God in **impersonal** terms. Maybe God is simply an idea: the idea of infinity; or the idea of prime number (which cannot be reduced or divided). God is, perhaps, a force, like magnetism or gravity, which invisibly influences the Earth. Maybe God is 'goodness' or 'light'. This impersonal God is closer to what many Christians believe, but there are problems here too. A person cannot have a relationship with a force.

In reality, Christians need both ideas to do justice to what they believe about God. At different times they emphasise one aspect rather than another.

Immanent or transcendent?

These two terms are usually used together as opposites.

An **immanent** God is 'in the world or the universe'. Most Christians believe that God has acted in human history in the past, is able to do so in the present and will do so again in the future. For this, God must be in the world. The prayers of many Christians assume an immanent God.

However, the problem with immanence is that it can limit God. Former Archbishop of Canterbury Robert Runcie launched an attack on 'informal' or personal worship and prayer saying such worship reduces God to the status of a puppet – whose role is to do whatever we want. For some Christians, an immanent God is too small.

Balanced against immanence, therefore, is the idea of **transcendence**. A transcendent God is 'outside or beyond the world or the universe', not limited in space or time and not able to act in space or time. Action is the responsibility of individual Christians on God's behalf. This idea is expressed in the prayer of St Teresa of Avila (Source D on page 60) – 'God has no hands but ours'.

A transcendent God best describes the faith of the many Christians who see no evidence of God acting in this world. God is remote and separate from human existence. God cares, but takes no active part in human life.

In practice, Christianity rejects extremes of either view. These concepts may be opposites, but they do not exclude each other.

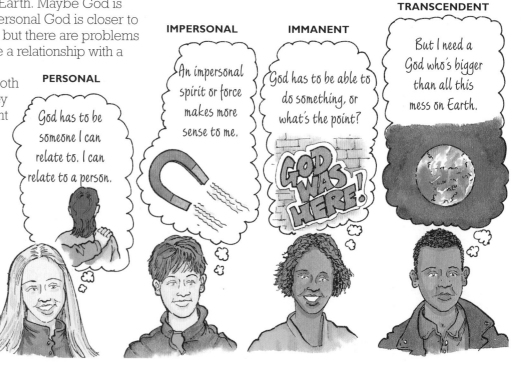

PERSONAL — God has to be someone I can relate to. I can relate to a person.

IMPERSONAL — An impersonal spirit or force makes more sense to me.

IMMANENT — God has to be able to do something, or what's the point? GOD WAS HERE!

TRANSCENDENT — But I need a God who's bigger than all this mess on Earth.

1   Which of these four ideas can you see in Sources A–D on pages 100–101?

✓ CHECKPOINT

Personal or impersonal? Immanent or transcendent? Each belief about the nature of God has an opposite. It is likely that for every person who holds the one view there will be one who holds the opposite view. God is like that! Then there will be others who will say that both ideas are true at the same time, even if they are conflicting ideas. This is because religious writing is often an attempt to describe the indescribable. So opposites and contradictions are sometimes quite helpful.

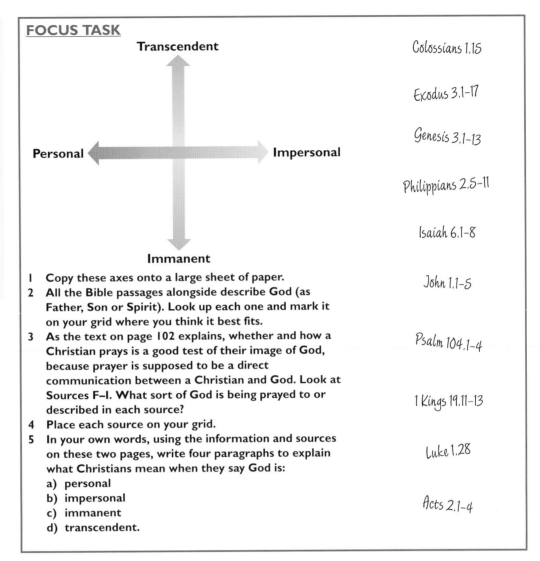

FOCUS TASK

Colossians 1.15

Exodus 3.1–17

Genesis 3.1–13

Philippians 2.5–11

Isaiah 6.1–8

John 1.1–5

Psalm 104.1–4

1 Kings 19.11–13

Luke 1.28

Acts 2.1–4

1   Copy these axes onto a large sheet of paper.
2   All the Bible passages alongside describe God (as Father, Son or Spirit). Look up each one and mark it on your grid where you think it best fits.
3   As the text on page 102 explains, whether and how a Christian prays is a good test of their image of God, because prayer is supposed to be a direct communication between a Christian and God. Look at Sources F–I. What sort of God is being prayed to or described in each source?
4   Place each source on your grid.
5   In your own words, using the information and sources on these two pages, write four paragraphs to explain what Christians mean when they say God is:
 a) personal
 b) impersonal
 c) immanent
 d) transcendent.

F

I often find myself talking to the Lord as I am driving. I keep my eyes open! But it is like having God in the car and feels perfectly natural, though I have received some strange looks at traffic lights from fellow road-users who imagine that I am talking to myself.

Dave Pope, evangelical leader

G

In the beginning was God,
Today is God,
Tomorrow will be God.
Who can make an image of God?
He has no body,
He is the word that comes out of your mouth.
That word! It is no more,
It is past, and still it lives!
So is God.

A prayer of the African Pygmy people

H

Risen Lord, King of Kings, Gentle Messiah, we worship you.
Break down the gates of every hell on Earth,
so that the light of your truth
may penetrate our darkened world.

Sheila Cassidy, campaigner for the hospice movement, tortured whilst a missionary in Chile

I

Glory be to you, Lord God, King of the universe;
Glory be to you, Lord God, dwelling in light and majesty;
Glory be to you, Lord God, beyond our highest thoughts;
Glory be to you, Lord God, giver of light and life.
Glory be to you from the company of heaven who see you face to face.

Neil Dixon

The Trinity

Most Christians believe that God has three persons, which they call Father, Son and Holy Spirit.

> The Father – the transcendent – 'God beyond us' who created the world and keeps it going.

> Jesus, the Son – the immanent and personal – 'God beside us' who came to earth and lived a human life.

J

God the Father, *God beyond us, we adore you.*
You are the depth of all that is.
You are the ground of our being.
We can never grasp you, yet you grasp us;
the universe speaks of you to us, and your love comes to us through Jesus.
God the Son, *God beside us, we adore you.*
You are the perfection of humanity.
You have shown us what human life should be like.
In you we see divine love and human greatness combined.
God the Spirit, *God around us, we adore you.*
You draw us to Jesus and the Father.
You are power within us.
You have given us abundant life and can make us
the men and women we are meant to be.
Father, Son, and Spirit;
God, beyond, beside and around us;
We adore you.

A prayer for Trinity Sunday by Caryl Mickelm, from the *SPCK Book of Christian Prayer*

K

... Jesus came from Nazareth in the province of Galilee, and was baptized by John in the Jordan. As soon as Jesus came up out of the water, he saw heaven opening and the Spirit coming down on him like a dove. And a voice came from heaven, 'You are my own dear Son. I am pleased with you.'

An account of Jesus' baptism (Mark 1.9–11)

> The Spirit – the immanent yet impersonal – 'God around us' who inspires and guides Christians from day to day.

1. List all the things that Sources J–M are saying about:
   a) the Father
   b) the Son
   c) the Spirit.
2. Where would you put the characteristics of each person of the Trinity on your grid from page 103?

FOCUS TASK

1. **Working with a partner discuss how the artists who made Sources L and M have tried to show the Trinity. In your discussions focus on the use of shape, colour, symbols, words and space.**
2. **Which do you think is the more successful representation?**
3. **Choose one image and write a 100-word summary of the Christian idea of the Trinity which could be displayed alongside the image in an exhibition of Christian art.**

One God or many?

MONOTHEISM is believing in one God. POLYTHEISM is believing in more than one god. Over the centuries Christian belief in the Trinity has caused much confusion. Critics say that Christians really believe in three gods. Christians say not.

> Why don't you come clean and admit that Christians believe in three gods?

> Because we don't! Christianity is a monotheistic religion, just like Islam and Judaism.

> Well how do you explain 'the Trinity' – God the Father, God the Son and God the Holy Spirit'?

> Trinity doesn't mean three gods, but one God in three persons. It makes better sense if you say 'God who is Father, Son and Holy Spirit'.

> So is it really just three aspects of God?

> Not exactly! Some Christians explain it like this: a person can be mother, sister and daughter at the same time. These are different relationships and roles, but the same person. Others compare the Trinity to ice, water and steam – the same substance in three forms. Others would say both those comparisons are quite misleading. That there is one God, but known in three persons.

L

Part of a wallpainting showing the Trinity by Masaccio, painted in 1427–8

M

A modern painting of the Trinity by John Piper, in Chichester Cathedral

Jesus

Jesus Christ is at the centre of Christian faith. The term 'Christian' means 'follower of Christ'. Let's examine a few of the basic beliefs that Christians have about Jesus.

Jesus is both fully God and fully human

Christians who believe in the Trinity believe that Jesus was God in a human body. They use the word 'incarnation' to describe this. Incarnation means becoming flesh. The festival of Christmas is a celebration of the incarnation – of God coming to Earth as a person.

The incarnation is deeply significant to Christians because it shows that God takes an active role in the lives of people. God becomes accessible and approachable, i.e. immanent and personal. In Jesus, God lived a totally human life. One of Jesus' other names is Immanuel, which means 'God with us.' In Jesus, God was most immanent: in the world, a part of the world, yet influencing it.

Jesus' death resolves the problem of sin

If Jesus was God in human form then his death also has particular importance. God is eternal, so God cannot die. So why did Jesus die? One common Christian explanation is that Jesus' death was part of God's plan for removing sin. All people fall short of God's standards; the fair punishment for this would be death. However, Jesus, who was both God and the only truly sinless human who ever lived, has taken the punishment on behalf of all people. God's forgiveness is, therefore, available to anyone. This is what Christians mean when they say that Christ is the 'Redeemer' or 'Saviour' of the world.

Jesus' resurrection resolves the problem of death

Jesus did not stay dead. He rose from death and returned to his Father for eternity. The same gift of eternal life is available to his followers (see page 124).

Jesus' teaching and example guide Christians in their daily lives

Jesus Christ is the perfect example of God-like attitudes and behaviour. Through the Gospels, Jesus' sermons, parables, miracles and actions show Christians how they should live.

N

I believe in God, the Father almighty, creator of heaven and Earth.

I believe in Jesus Christ, his only Son, our Lord. He was conceived by the power of the Holy Spirit and born of the Virgin Mary. He suffered under Pontius Pilate, was crucified, died, and was buried. He descended to the dead. On the third day he rose again. He ascended into heaven, and is seated at the right hand of the Father. He will come again to judge the living and the dead.

I believe in the Holy Spirit, the holy Catholic Church, the communion of saints, the forgiveness of sins, the resurrection of the body, and the life everlasting. Amen.

The *Apostles' Creed*. Early Christian leaders drew up such creeds (statements of belief) to summarise Christian beliefs. This creed, from the 4th century is still said in many Christian churches every Sunday.

ACTIVITY A

Every time Christians recite the *Apostles' Creed* (Source N) they restate their most basic beliefs about Jesus.
1 Draw up a table like the one below.
2 Look at the middle paragraph of Source N. Write each claim about Jesus in the appropriate column of your table.

Jesus as a human being	Jesus as God
He was born to a human mother	His mother was a virgin

3 How do you think a creed like this, written more than 1,500 years ago, is useful to Christians today?

SAVE AS ...

4 Record in your own words what the word 'incarnation' means, and why it is important to Christians.

ACTIVITY B

1 Source O is based on a story from the Gospels.
  a) Read the story in John 8.1-11.
  b) Discuss with a partner what attitude each of the characters is showing towards Jesus.
  c) Do people today have similar or different attitudes towards Jesus to the characters in Source O.

2 Source P is a carnival float. It was not intended as a comment on Jesus, but imagine it was.
  • 'This is a good symbol of Jesus' presence in the world. He is surrounded by all the mess humans create, yet he is serene and rising above it.'
  • 'This is a poor symbol of Jesus' presence in the world. He is surrounded by the world but he is helpless, carried along by forces beyond his control.'
  a) Which of these two speakers do you agree with more? Explain your choice.
  b) If you agree with the second speaker, redesign the carnival float to better express the idea of incarnation.

3 Imagine you have to make a six-frame story strip of Jesus' life for someone who knows almost nothing about it. Using your own background knowledge, decide what your six frames ought to show. What aspects of Jesus will you focus on? You could use the middle paragraph of the creed in Source N to help you, or you could look up these Bible references:
  • Matthew 1.18–25
  • Matthew 5.1–10
  • Matthew 14.13–21 and 22–31
  • Matthew 21.12–13
  • Matthew 26.26–30
  • Matthew 27.32–50
  • Matthew 28.1–10

O

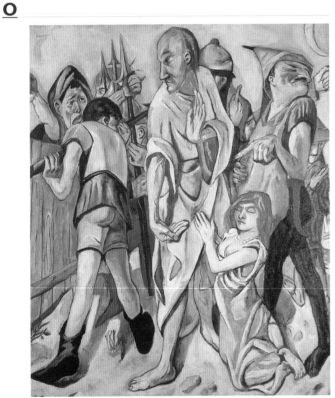

Christ and the woman taken in adultery by Max Beckman. This picture is based on a story in John 8.1–11.

P

A copy of the statue of *Christ the Redeemer*, which stands above Rio de Janiero, used as part of a carnival float in Brazil

FOCUS TASK

'A God we can understand is no God at all'
This was said by St John Chrysostom 1,600 years ago.
Do you agree with what St John said?
  Write an essay which explores this question. Make use of all the material you have read on pages 100–107.

5.4 One God ... revealed in many ways

The illustration shows some of the ways in which Christians believe God is revealed to humans.

Step inside the theme park. What do you find?

A

Earth is crammed with heaven
And every common bush is afire with God.
But only he who sees takes off his shoes;
The rest sit round and pluck blackberries.

Elizabeth Barrett Browning,
English poet (1806–61)

Christians believe that some things about God can be known through the **natural world**. The Old Testament psalm writers said, 'The Earth proclaims God's glory.' On page 94 you saw how some Christians interpret God's character through the natural world. However, few Christians would claim this form of revelation is enough on its own (see Source A). Most Christians would agree that nature reveals God, but only to the searchers.

So, where to next? If you want to get to know someone, you go to see them, talk to them, ask them questions. To get to know God, the logical thing would be to do the same: meet God, ask questions, have a chat (see Source B). Unfortunately, God is not like that! But there are other ways.

B

Wouldn't it be fantastic, and so much easier for people like me who don't really know, if God just came in, sat down here with us and offered me a cigarette or poured me a cup of coffee. Then everyone would know and I could say, 'It's all right. I've seen him. It's fine. Relax. Join in.'

Television comedienne Caroline Quentin, talking to Anglican Bishop Roy Williamson

> 1 **Explain how two different traditions use the term 'Word of God'.**

The Bible gives the searcher a much clearer image of the Christian God and how this God is different from other gods. It tells the story of God's relationship with humans, from the Earth's Creation to the founding of the Christian Church. It suggests that, far from Christianity being about people searching for God, it is about God searching for people. Christians call this God's SELF-REVELATION.

Some evangelical Christians claim that the Bible is so complete a revelation that it is all you need. They call the Bible the 'Word of God'. Others argue that God's revelation did not stop in the first century of the Christian Era. However, for Catholics, the Word of God is a combination of the Bible and **Church teachings**. Church teachings, which have been developed over 2,000 years of Christian history, are part of God's revelation. The Catholic Christian needs to know both in order to find out about and follow God.

If you tried all these things, you would have a fairly clear idea of basic Christian ideas about God. However, you might feel these types of revelation are too impersonal. They might seem general, distant and second-hand. You could keep on coming back for more. After all, the human mind is limited and cannot take everything in at once. Each time you looked at these sources of revelation you might understand God more deeply. However, you might still need more. You *know about* God, but have you met God? Where do you go for something more direct?

Some find God is revealed through the lives of **great Christians**. These people seem closer to God than ordinary people. They understand more of God, and searchers can meet God through them and learn from their successes and failures. They can copy them and be inspired by them.

Others find God through **Christian worship**. The symbols, music, sights and sounds open up the worshipper to God's revelation. And when you worship with other Christians, even the drier aspects of revelation seem to speak more directly.

Is that enough to know God? Some would say it is. Others would say, 'If I am really going to know God I need direct revelation: to hear God calling me or talking to me in person, giving me messages, answering my prayers, moving me emotionally, making me feel right with God.' They would search for a **personal experience**. We examine this on pages 98–9 and 112.

FOCUS TASK

1 Which, if any, of these rides would you most like to try?
2 Using the text to help you, write a brief description of how each of the following 'rides' can reveal God to Christians:
   a) the natural world
   b) the Bible
   c) Church teachings
   d) Religious leaders.
   Use examples from earlier in this book.
3 Is God revealed in other ways? What might be in the mystery ride? Write a description of the ride to add to the theme park.
4 Why do you think God is revealed in so many different ways?

Key questions for Christians

• How is God revealed?
• How do Christians find out about God?
• Do religious experiences reveal God?

How do Christians find out the will of God?

One important aspect of revelation is how Christians can find out the will of God. Can they only find out God's will in a general way – rough guidelines for their situation – or can they get specific guidance? If so, how? This is an issue you have already encountered in Units 1–4.

Here are two case studies, from different traditions, at different scales, on different issues. Let's see how God's will was revealed in each case.

Case study 1: Jonathan Edwards – revelation on a small scale

Should I jump on a Sunday?

In 1992 he began to reconsider.

Until 1992, world champion triple-jumper Jonathan Edwards had never jumped on a Sunday because his Christian faith made him believe that Sunday was a holy day of worship and that he should keep Sunday special. This was a very public stance. Some admired him for it. Some thought he was a bit misguided.

My initial decision not to jump on a Sunday was a big one. I love my athletics, but knew that God was calling me to make a stand for him, to show my priorities. The issue was never whether it was right or wrong to jump on a Sunday – rather, was it right for me?

✓ CHECKPOINT
Types of revelation

GENERAL REVELATION is indirect and available to everyone. This term is particularly used to describe the way God's character is revealed through the natural world or through reason, conscience or moral sense.

SPECIAL REVELATION is direct revelation to an individual or group. Something new about God might be revealed through, for example, a dream, vision, prophecy or experience.

Some would argue that general revelation is everything people need in order to know God. If God is eternal and does not change, so God's revelation must be unchanging. Other people believe that if God is immanent and actively intervening in history, God should also be expected to give new and special revelation to each generation.

Most Christians believe that the two forms of revelation need to be balanced.

Your exam might ask you to explain whether the Bible is an example of general or special revelation. The majority of Christians regard the Bible as a form of special revelation. The Holy Spirit gave the writers unique insights which could not have been known any other way. However, there is another view. Some Christians would say that the Bible simply records human experiences as they search for God. It therefore *contains* examples of God communicating through both special and general revelation.

In 1992 I felt a freedom to start jumping on a Sunday. I started to pray about it and shared with Christian friends the feeling that God was calling me to jump on Sundays. However, at the end of the season the urgency I felt concerning this subsided and I decided to continue with my former stance.

Then, when I found out that all the major competitions in 1993 would be on Sundays I was stunned. I knew God was calling me to serve him as an athlete . . . yet here he was slamming the door in my face.

That evening I felt God telling me to visit a friend, who told me of a dream he'd had about me. I was at the end of the runway waiting to jump, but I was frustrated by many people in my way; when the people were moved I ran down and made a great leap. It felt that God was saying to me, through this dream, that it was fear of man that was stopping me deciding to jump on Sundays. Humanly, I can see many good and persuasive arguments to not jump on Sunday, yet God wants us to walk by faith and not by sight.

Much of my wisdom tells me: don't do it. Yet God's Word says: 'Trust in the Lord with all your heart. Never rely on what you think you know. Remember the Lord in everything you do, and he will show you the right way.' (Proverbs 3.5–6)

I now believe God is calling me to serve him by competing on any day of the week.

<u>C</u>ase study 2: *Vatican 2 – revelation on an epic scale*

How can the Catholic Church be relevant to the modern world?

The Catholic Church is the biggest Christian tradition (see page 7). It is strong in every continent. The social changes of the 20th century have put great pressure on the Catholic Church, as on many other institutions, to adapt to meet the needs of the modern world. In the 1960s the Catholic Church met to reconsider Catholic doctrine on the main issues.

It was the best prepared council ever … 800 theologians prepared the agenda … 2,500 bishops and leaders and 37 Catholic universities were asked what they thought were the major problems facing the Church … Twelve preparatory commissions were set up. The central one included the Pope. Seventy draft documents were prepared for the commissions to consider.

Catholic historian Michael Walsh describing *Vatican 2*

At the Council, Pope John XXIII first established the rules of procedure – who was there to advise and who to make decisions. Each day began with a Mass. Then a general congregation of hundreds of bishops met to discuss each draft document. Conservatives and modernisers argued with each other. Should Latin continue to be used for the Mass or should local languages be used? Should Catholics be encouraged to study the Bible more than they did? Could Catholics work more closely with other Churches? Should Catholics be allowed to use contraception?

Each draft document was debated and sent back to the commissions for changes while the Council members returned to their main jobs. For four years, they returned each summer and autumn to look at new topics: racism, marriage, discrimination against women, even tourism and television, as well as theological topics such as revelation.

After four years of drafting, debate and redrafting by thousands of Catholic leaders, the 16 documents which came out of *Vatican 2* were agreed. In all cases, the *Vatican 2* documents carefully explained their judgements by reference to the Bible and earlier Catholic teaching. These documents were sent to the Catholic churches around the world to guide their development.

On some issues, *Vatican 2* re-emphasised the traditional teaching of the Church; on others it established a radically new agenda for Catholics. It led to many significant changes in the Catholic Church.

ACTIVITY

Work in pairs. Take one case study each.
1 **List all the different types of revelation which helped guide the decision making.**
2 **Compare your lists. Are there any common elements?**

SAVE AS …

3 **Read the Checkpoint on page 110 and record in your own words the meaning of the terms 'General revelation' and 'Special revelation'. Use examples from the last four pages.**

Experiences of God

God is revealed to ordinary Christians through religious experiences. On these pages, four kinds of religious experience that can reveal more about God to the believer are described.

Conversion

Conversion means becoming a follower of God.

The Bible contains spectacular examples of conversion: Moses was called by God from a burning bush (Exodus 3); Saul (Acts 9) was on his way to break up a Christian meeting when he was called by a voice from heaven.

In the modern evangelical tradition, conversion has a special significance. It is seen as the entry point to faith. To be converted is much more important, for example, than being baptised; a person has to admit their sins to God and ask for God's forgiveness. Some evangelicals call this being 'born again' or 'saved'. An important feature at evangelical meetings is often a call for people to come forward and commit their lives to God. However, conversion happens within all traditions. It can result from meditation, prayer or reading.

Some people's conversion is a physical experience. They may cry uncontrollably or feel dizzy or weak at the knees. Some people feel afraid, some indescribably happy. Conversions might coincide with another experience. Sick people have found themselves healed at their conversion (see page 98, for example). Many people find that conversion changes the direction of their lives forever. It changes their relationships with family and friends. For some Christians, conversion is the most important religious experience in their life. They look back to it in later years as the time when God's nature or God's will or God's attitudes were revealed specially to them. They felt that God loved them personally or had a plan for their lives.

C

One dark wintry afternoon I was sitting alone in my study at school. I suddenly became aware of a figure in white whom I saw pretty clearly in my mind's eye. I heard the words, 'Follow me'. Instinctively I knew that this was Jesus. Heaven knows how – I knew nothing about him.

It was an indescribably rich event that filled me afterwards with overpowering joy. I could do no other than follow those instructions.

Extract from the autobiography of Bishop Hugh Montefiore. He was born a Jew and was 16 at the time of this experience. He went on to become an Anglican bishop.

Charismatic worship

Some Christians find that after conversion they have a later experience of 'Baptism in the Spirit'. They feel God's Holy Spirit touching them and changing them. They are more aware of God's presence. They are set free to worship God in an uninhibited way. They are given spiritual gifts, such as speaking in tongues (other languages or strange sounds), prophesying (receiving messages to pass on to others) or having visions. These spiritual gifts are called CHARISMATA and they are a central feature of charismatic worship. When worshippers feel close to God they might sing, pray, dance, hold their arms in the air, laugh, cry or shake uncontrollably. There may be words of knowledge or healings (see page 98). Many find that charismatic worship gives them a new sense of God's presence and power.

In John 14.15–16 Jesus promised his disciples that, when he was taken away from them, he would send another 'Comforter' to them: his Holy Spirit. The first Christians experienced the first baptism in the Holy Spirit on the Day of Pentecost (Acts 2). Charismatic worship was central to the first Christians. It was controversial, even then, and many of the letters of Paul deal with how to use these spiritual gifts correctly (see, for example, 1 Corinthians 12.1–11).

Controversy has surrounded the issue of spiritual gifts ever since. Early this century, the Pentecostal Church grew out of a revival of this kind of worship. More recently, the Charismatic Movement introduced the use of spiritual gifts into mainstream churches in the 1960s. Some churches rejected charismatic worship, regarding it as mass hysteria whipped up by worship leaders. Others embraced it, believing spiritual gifts were the most basic form of spiritual revelation – the way for God to communicate directly with people. They pointed to the example of the earliest Christians. The House Church movement started as people left mainstream denominations for new independent churches where they could hold charismatic worship.

Today, charismatic worship is much more accepted. There is now a strong Charismatic movement within the mainstream Protestant, Catholic and Orthodox traditions.

D

One recent form of charismatic revival is called the Toronto Blessing since it started in Toronto, Canada.

The Eucharist

At the Eucharist (Communion) worshippers take bread and wine. These are symbols of Jesus' body and blood. The Eucharist is one of the seven SACRAMENTS used by Christian Churches. A sacrament is 'an outward sign of an inward grace', which means a ritual to feed Christian faith.

Jesus initiated the Eucharist. He said to his disciples at their last meal together, 'This is my body which is given for you. Do this in memory of me.' (Luke 22.19). The Eucharist is a central feature of worship in the Catholic and Orthodox traditions and in many Protestant churches.

For many Christians the experience of taking the Eucharist is the focus of their religious life. As prayers are said and songs are sung, the bread is given to each individual with the words: 'This is the body of Christ – feed on him in your hearts.' Some worshippers believe the bread and wine become the actual body and blood of Christ. Others believe the elements are symbols. In either case, the Eucharist celebrates the presence of Christ in the world and in a Christian's life. It is a physical reminder that Jesus is on Earth. It gains special significance from being an experience shared with millions of other Christians all over the world, from a massive open-air Mass with hundreds of thousands of other Christians to a simple service for the housebound (see photograph).

A Christian's first Eucharist is a rite of passage. People prepare carefully for it. Those who are not ready to take Communion often come forward for a blessing by the priest. In the Orthodox Church even babies are brought to Communion.

Meditation

Meditation means focusing on God. As Christians focus on God, blocking out all distractions, they receive revelation from God. They may see visions or hear voices.

Meditation can take place anywhere – in a church, in the countryside, at home or school in the middle of a busy day. It can involve reading the Bible, praying or fasting (going without food).

Some meditate by cutting themselves off from other humans. Jesus prayed and meditated in the desert as part of his preparation for his teaching ministry. Dame Julian of Norwich was a 14th-century recluse. She lived alone in a cell meditating on God and offering spiritual advice to people who passed by. In her most famous vision, God showed her a hazelnut in the palm of her hand. It seemed so vulnerable that she asked God how it survived. She was answered: 'It lasts and always will because God loves it.' In the same way, she said, everything exists through the love of God.

In his famous *The Practice of the Presence of God* Brother Roger (born 1915) suggested a different approach to meditation. He aimed to focus so totally on whatever he was doing – whether cutting a vegetable or washing dishes – that God was able to speak to him through that activity.

E

A Quaker meeting. Worship in this tradition is built around silent meditation as a group. 'In a meeting, friends gather in silence as seeking souls … Often, out of that silence is born the message of that meeting, expressed, it may be, by several speakers and yet with a central thought' (*Quaker Faith and Practice*, paragraph 234).

FOCUS TASK

Draw up a table like this:

Experience	Example	What it reveals about God	I think it is illusion or reality because …

1 Complete the table using the information panels.
2 How are the experiences similar?
3 How do the experiences differ?
4 Churches that emphasise conversion and charismatic worship are among the fastest growing in the UK and worldwide. Why do you think this might be?

5.5   Why do people suffer?

A

They were in the school gym when the gunman opened fire. Three minutes later 16 children lay dying

… it seems that the teacher died trying to shield her pupils from the bullets. In his final act, Thomas Hamilton, 43, who was forced to quit the Scouts amid abuse allegations, turned the gun on himself and committed suicide.

ACTIVITY

1   Read the views expressed in Source B. Choose two statements which you agree with and two which you disagree with and explain your choice.
2   Who was to blame for the Dunblane massacre? Explain your answer carefully.
3   Many schools across Britain responded to the Dunblane tragedy by sending flowers, cards and letters. Write a short note to the headteacher of the school expressing your reaction.

B

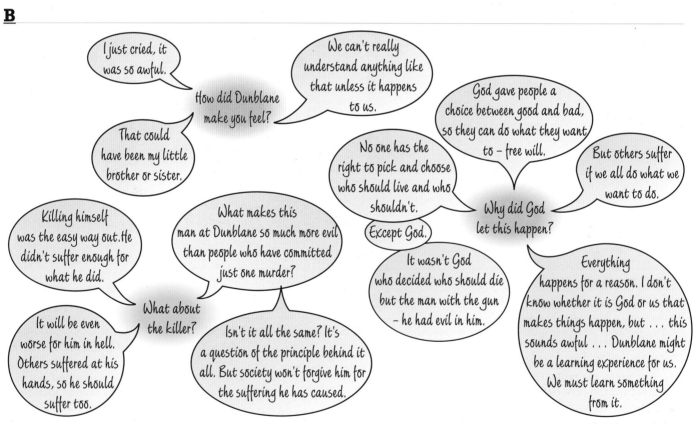

Extracts from a taped discussion at a school Christian Union meeting a few days after the Dunblane massacre in 1996. The participants included Anglicans, Catholics and Baptists.

<u>W</u>hy?

The Dunblane massacre was a national tragedy. This cold-blooded, pre-meditated killing touched a nerve throughout Britain. The first reaction, not surprisingly, was shock and horror at 16 innocent lives destroyed. The next was to seek explanations. The police were asked about where the killer got his guns. The psychologists were asked about the mentality of mass murder. Church leaders were asked difficult questions like 'Why does God allow such suffering and evil in this world?'.

C

On the television that evening an agonised Dean of the Cathedral made a deeply sincere impression when he admitted that it was impossible to provide any immediate reasoning that could make sense of what had happened, or that could offer any proper consolation to the bereaved. But I am sure the Church did itself considerable damage the next morning when it allowed some cocksure vicar on the 'Today' programme [news and comment on Radio 4] to go on and piously assert that 'God has a special place for little children'.

David Hare, British playwright, speaking to Anglican Church leaders some months after the Dunblane massacre

<u>K</u>ey questions for Christians

* Why does God allow suffering to happen?
* Where does evil come from?
* How can Christians help those who are suffering?

D

'Don't blame me! I just work in his advertising department'

FOCUS TASK

1. • Natural suffering is suffering that is caused by events beyond human control.
   • Human-made suffering is suffering that is caused by human actions.

   Explain whether each headline in **Source D** is an example of natural suffering or human-made suffering.

2. In groups, brainstorm as many other examples of suffering as you can think of. Write each one on a separate slip of paper. Then on a larger sheet of paper sort them into categories. First try sorting them into natural and human-made suffering. Then devise your own sub-categories. Your teacher can give you suggestions if you are stuck, for example: human greed, human error.

SAVE AS ...

Write a paragraph to explain your own view on the following questions:
a) Where does evil come from?
b) Why does God allow suffering to happen?

Christian perspectives on suffering

Suffering is an old problem for religious believers, particularly for those who believe that God is all-powerful, all-knowing, all-loving. Source E summarises the problem.

E

People suffer, so ...	Maybe God doesn't care about human suffering, or is even causing the human suffering → Maybe God isn't all-loving
Maybe God can't do anything about human suffering → Maybe God isn't all-powerful	Maybe there isn't a God after all.
Maybe God doesn't know about human suffering → Maybe God isn't all-knowing	

Case study: the suffering of Job

The Bible contains many examples of human suffering: natural disasters, slavery, wars, refugee crises, persecution, plagues, mass murder, genocide, executions. They affect the good as well as the bad. They affect God's followers as much as their enemies. So naturally the Bible wrestles with exactly the same questions as those in Source E.

One whole book of the Old Testament – Job – is devoted to the problem of suffering. Job (rhymes with globe) is a good man who suffers total disaster. His children are killed, he loses all his property and possessions and he is afflicted by a painful and disfiguring skin disease.

The bulk of the book of Job is made up of conversations between Job, his friends and God. The book offers three possible explanations for Job's suffering (see Source F).

F

Idea 1: Suffering is a test
God is allowing Satan to test Job to see if he deserts God. When, despite his suffering, Job does not lose his faith in God, he is rewarded.

Idea 2: Suffering is a punishment for sin
Job's friends are very keen on this idea. They tell Job he must have sinned greatly to suffer so much. They encourage him to search his life for unconfessed sins and to repent. Job protests that he has always been faithful and good.

When God eventually speaks, God rejects the second idea, and accuses Job's friends of being wrong-minded. God introduces the third idea instead.

Idea 3: Suffering is part of God's plan, which is beyond human understanding
Humans just have to accept what they cannot understand. God does not say what the plan is; we never know – but Job seems satisfied! And he's healed, and his wealth is restored to him!

Who are you to question my wisdom with your ignorant empty words?

G

Try to exclude the possibility of suffering which the order of nature and existence of free will involve, and you find you have excluded life itself.

C.S. Lewis was a Christian writer whose wife died of cancer less than two years after they married

---

SAVE AS ...

Using the text on this page, explain in your own words what C.S Lewis meant in Source G.

H

Suffering Christ by Nikolai Nikolaevich (1831–94)

Why does God not prevent suffering?

Since Job, many Christian writers have attempted to explain suffering. They have often concluded that suffering is an inevitable part of being human.

Free will

Christians believe that God gives people free will. They live their lives as they choose. If God interfered every time people did something that would cause harm to themselves or others then people would be puppets of God. Without free will there would be no point to their lives. God has shown how people should live. Humans decide whether or not to follow God's instructions. They take the consequences of their decisions.

Genesis 1–3 suggests that the world was once without suffering. Then Adam (of his own free will) ate fruit that God had forbidden him. God punished Adam's disobedience with pain and hard work. Irrespective of whether Christians believe this story is literally true, it is still retold to illustrate how humans with free will have a tendency towards not doing what God wants them to do. Much suffering can be traced back to human failings.

The balance of nature

The world is a carefully balanced whole. All parts are intricately related. But the world itself is not moral. The world does not only do good things. Rather, it is a world in which certain natural (amoral) laws determine everything that happens.

So natural processes can produce good and bad effects. The flood which kills some people waters the land which allows other to live. The earthquake which destroys a city is caused by the forces that created the land on which we are able to live.

Christians believe that we view the world from a very lowly point. If we could gain a higher God-type vantage point we would see that every living thing is part of a finely balanced whole; that all physical processes are part of a system. God sets the world going, then leaves it to follow its natural course. It would be wrong for God to intervene. This would disrupt the laws of nature. How would God decide when to act and when not to? How could God choose between the suffering of one group of people and the well-being of another?

Insurance policies refer to earthquakes and floods as 'acts of God', but really they are acts of nature which God chooses not to control.

The suffering of Jesus

As if to confirm that suffering is a necessary part of being human, Christians also point to the suffering of Jesus who, as a man, suffered greatly.

As Jesus prayed before his death, he said, 'The sorrow in my heart is so great that it almost crushes me.' (Mark 14.34). He was executed in an excruciatingly painful way, by crucifixion. Just before he died, he shouted out, 'My God, my God, why did you abandon me?' (Mark 15.34).

He also said, 'It is accomplished!' (John 19.30), suggesting that his suffering had a purpose.

Christian perspectives on evil

'No words can express the shock and sorrow brought about by this mad and evil act.' This was the reaction of Prime Minister John Major to the Dunblane massacre. There was a great deal of talk about evil in the weeks following. A parent at the school said, 'Today we have been visited by evil.' The students from page 114 were also asked about evil. You can read their views in Source I.

I

Anita: His own past experiences put evil in the killer's mind.

Alex: There is good and there is evil. God can bring good into the world – he did so at Creation – but he can't be responsible for evil.

Richard: We all have different emotions – hate, love and so on – they can be used for good or bad. That is how evil gets into the world, it is the way that people use their emotions. To hate my teacher would be wrong, but to hate Hitler is all right because it is a response to his actions.

Felicity: You can't blame the evil in the world on Satan, we have to accept that we have evil in us – it goes back to original sin and free will, but that's the easy way out.

Rohan: Satan was head angel and thought he was better than God and wanted people to worship him, and so God kicked him out of heaven. If God is pulling the strings for good, then surely Satan is pulling the strings for bad or evil on earth. We choose which we allow to control us.

Helen: We all have an element of badness in us, but it is only when the bad overtakes the good that we start to become evil and sinful.

FOCUS TASK

1 Copy a simplified version of the diagram on the right onto a sheet of A3 paper.
2 Study Source I. Write each student's name on a slip of paper.
3 With a partner, place each slip of paper in an appropriate place on your diagram, according to that student's belief about where evil comes from. You might disagree about where to place them. You might need to adapt the diagram or add new headings.
4 Add your own name in an appropriate place to show what you believe.
5 Record in your own words the three different explanations of evil as:
   • a person
   • a force
   • a psychological phenomenon.

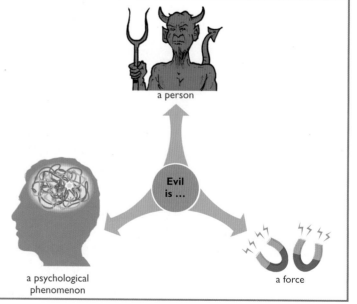

a person

Evil is …

a psychological phenomenon

a force

DISCUSS

One event which has influenced the whole perception of evil is the Holocaust, when millions of people, including six million Jews, died in Nazi concentration camps.

The Holocaust required the involvement of a great many individuals, from the soldier who rounded up the victims to the scientist perfecting Zyklon B, the chemical that killed millions of innocent people in the gas chambers.

Intentional suffering on such a massive scale raised very basic questions about human morality and evil. Is it enough to say that Hitler and other Nazi leaders were warped individuals?

1 Which view of evil best explains the Holocaust:
   • original sin
   • absence of good
   • Satan
   • warped minds?
2 Which view best explains Dunblane?
3 'All that is needed for evil to triumph is for good people to do nothing.' Do you agree?

A brief history of evil

Original sin

Genesis 3 begins with the story of the first sin. According to one view of evil, 'the fall' of Adam and Eve introduced sin into the world, and since then all people have been born with a tendency towards evil. This is called 'ORIGINAL SIN'. It means the tendency to evil is in everyone. One assumption throughout the Bible is that evil comes from human failings.

Absence of good

In the fourth century, St Augustine suggested a different view. He said that evil was 'absence of good'. All things were created good, but because of free will it was possible for things to grow away from good and become evil. However, he added that what appears evil may be good in the context of eternity.

Satan

Satan is an ancient Middle Eastern word meaning 'an accuser'. Satan appears at various times through the Bible as the opposite to God. Satan, in the form of the snake, tempts Eve to eat the apple. Satan tests Job. Satan tempts Jesus to abandon his ministry.

In the Middle Ages the Church developed something of an obsession with Satan. Satan, or the Devil, was seen as an ugly man dressed in red, who lived in the fires of a place called hell. Life was pictured as a cosmic struggle between God and Satan, or Good and Evil in which humans were little more than pawns.

A medieval wall painting in Florence, Italy

This view still has influence in the modern world. There are Christians whose life revolves around 'resisting Satan'. They ban the music of rock groups whose lyrics supposedly include Satanic ideas. They hold exorcisms to rid people of Satanic influence.

A damaged mind

Today, evil is more usually seen as a psychological phenomenon. Evil is created by the psychological forces that shape our character – our parenting, our schooling, our diet, what we watch on television and in films. After the events of Dunblane the press immediately focused on Thomas Hamilton's parenting, friendships, magazines, videos, etc. to try to explain his behaviour. What forces had damaged his mind?

ACTIVITY

1 On your own copy of the diagram below, write each quotation on the right wherever you think it best belongs.

2 Imagine you are making a card for a **Christian** friend who has suffered in some way (you can decide how). Choose one quotation to use in your card. Say why you have chosen it. If none of the quotations appeals to you, explain why you have rejected them. Write your own message instead.

3 Design an appropriate picture for your card.

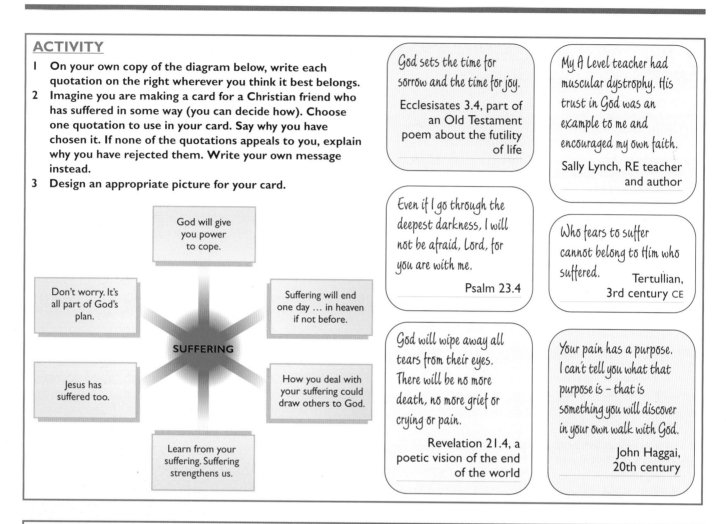

God will give you power to cope.

Don't worry. It's all part of God's plan.

Suffering will end one day … in heaven if not before.

SUFFERING

Jesus has suffered too.

How you deal with your suffering could draw others to God.

Learn from your suffering. Suffering strengthens us.

> God sets the time for sorrow and the time for joy.
> Ecclesiastes 3.4, part of an Old Testament poem about the futility of life

> My A Level teacher had muscular dystrophy. His trust in God was an example to me and encouraged my own faith.
> Sally Lynch, RE teacher and author

> Even if I go through the deepest darkness, I will not be afraid, Lord, for you are with me.
> Psalm 23.4

> Who fears to suffer cannot belong to Him who suffered.
> Tertullian, 3rd century CE

> God will wipe away all tears from their eyes. There will be no more death, no more grief or crying or pain.
> Revelation 21.4, a poetic vision of the end of the world

> Your pain has a purpose. I can't tell you what that purpose is – that is something you will discover in your own walk with God.
> John Haggai, 20th century

FOCUS TASK

1 Explain how Source L might give comfort to a Christian who was suffering.

2 Explain two other ways in which Christian faith might give 'hope and purpose' to someone who was suffering.

3 The priest in Source K talks about 'God's powerful love'. Explain in your own words how suffering can cause a Christian to question:
   a) God's love
   b) God's power.

4 Christians believe there are arguments to counter these doubts. How could the priest reply to each question?

5 'Pain and suffering are never the will of God.' Do you agree? Explain your view, showing that you have considered other points of view.

K

The Christian faith gives hope and purpose even in apparently hopeless situations. God's powerful love promises a future, and the security of continuing care and strength to us when we have none of our own.

Lis, a Church of England priest and chaplain to a hospice for terminally-ill children

L

Crucifixion by Andrei Mylnikov (born 1919)

5.6 What kind of future do Christians look forward to?

<u>W</u>hat lies beyond the grave?

Christians believe in life after death, although they don't all agree what form it might take. Sources A – D show some Christian points of view.

A

I believe that when the body dies, the soul lives on in a new life. It's like you plant a seed to make a new plant. The new plant is beautiful, but if you dig the seed up you will find it is all rotten and horrible. In our church we place a bowl of wheat grain on a table at funerals to remind us of this idea.

Anthony, an Orthodox Christian

B

My church used to teach that when you die you can't go straight to heaven because no one is perfect enough to come into the the presence of God. So you went to purgatory – a kind of halfway house where you could become perfect and ready to enter heaven itself. We do not hear that so much today, but the idea makes sense to me.

Keith, a Catholic priest in London

C

When my father died I was very sad, but I believe I will meet him one day in heaven. He was a Christian. I saw him praying just a few days before his death. I feel connected to him even now. Every week we say in the Creed 'I believe in the Communion of Saints' – that means the togetherness of all Christians, all over the world, living and dead.

Sarah, a teacher and a member of an Anglican church

D

Tombstones in a cemetery in Cambridgeshire

ACTIVITY

Source	What lies beyond the grave?

1 Draw up a table like this, then complete it to show the different beliefs about life after death expressed in **Sources A–D**.
2 What do they agree about?
3 What do they disagree about?

SAVE AS ...

4 Write a paragraph recording your own views about life after death.

Key questions for Christians

- Is there a heaven?
- If there is a heaven, who will go there?
- Can Christians bring the Kingdom of Heaven to this Earth?

Images of heaven

Although near-death experiences suggest that some sort of afterlife exists, no human being has ever been able to come back from death with an eye-witness account of heaven, and though the Bible often mentions heaven it is rarely described. So Christians have widely differing ideas about heaven.

E

Then I saw a new heaven and a new Earth. The first heaven and the first Earth disappeared, and the sea vanished. And I saw the Holy City, the new Jerusalem, coming down out of heaven from God, prepared and ready, like a bride dressed to meet her husband. I heard a loud voice speaking from the throne: 'Now God's home is with human beings! He will live with them, and they shall be his people. God himself will be with them, and he will be their God. He will wipe away all tears from their eyes. There will be no more death, no more grief or crying or pain. The old things have disappeared.'

Revelation 21.1–4

F

*Bring us, O Lord, at our last awakening
into the house and gate of heaven,
to enter into that gate and dwell in that house
where shall be no darkness nor dazzling,
but one equal light;
no noise nor silence,
but one equal music;
no fears nor hopes,
but one equal possession;
no ends nor beginnings,
but one equal eternity
in the habitations of your glory and dominion,
world without end.*

John Donne, an English poet (1573–1631)

G

Angels in a heavenly landscape, from a fresco by Benezzo di Lese di Sandro Gozzoli (1420–97)

✓ CHECKPOINT

What about hell?

The Bible is even less clear about hell than it is about heaven. The parable of the rich man and Lazarus (Luke 16.19–31) gives some idea of what early Christians believed happened to the souls of those who had behaved badly.

Descriptions of hell owed a lot to the valley of Gehenna, just outside Jerusalem. It was a rubbish tip, and had been the site of pagan child-sacrifices. Fires were always burning there. It was associated with bad things. From this, descriptions of hell gradually developed into the images we are familiar with today of terrible torture, fire and demons.

Some Christians believe strongly in hell and everlasting punishment for those who have committed terrible, violent crimes against others. Others have a far less clear idea. Some argue that God's saving power extends to all people, whatever sins they have committed.

H

Preacher, don't send me
when I die
to some big ghetto
in the sky
where rats eat cats
of the leopard type
and Sunday brunch
is grits and tripe.

I've known those rats
I've seen them kill
and grits I've had
would make a hill,
(or maybe a mountain)
so what I need
from you on Sunday
is a different creed.

Preacher, please don't
promise me
streets of gold
and milk for free.
I stopped all milk
at four years old
and once I'm dead
I won't need gold.

I'd call a place
pure paradise
where families are loyal
and strangers are nice,
where the music is jazz
and the season is fall.
Promise me that
or nothing at all.

Maya Angelou, from *I Shall Not Be Moved* (1990)

1 The parable of the rich man and Lazarus (Luke 16.19–31) is one of the few places in the Gospels where Jesus is a bit more more specific about heaven (and hell). Read the passage and note the images the story contains. How far do they match your own ideas about the afterlife?

FOCUS TASK

1 Make a list of all the words you associate with 'heaven'.
2 Compare your list with those of others in your class.
3 Which of your ideas can you see in Sources E–H?
4 With which of the images of heaven in Sources E–H do you most identify? Explain why.
5 Explain with which image you least identify.
6 Try to express your views about life after death using your own images and ideas.
  • You could draw a personal response to your preferred image.
  • You could research and find a source of your own and illustrate it with images from newspapers or magazines.
  • You could write an acrostic poem entitled 'Life After Death'. In an acrostic, the first letters of each line spell out the title.

Who will go to heaven?

Salvation is one of the most controversial topics in Christian theology. Christians would give a wide range of answers if asked, 'Who is saved by God?' or 'Who, if anyone, will go to heaven?' Jesus made it clear that it is not for human beings to judge who will be saved and who will not – only God can make such decisions (see Matthew 7.1-6, for example). Nevertheless, Christians have always discussed this issue. Some of the most common views can be found in Source I.

The significance of Jesus

You can see that what Christians believe about salvation and eternal life is closely related to what they believe about Jesus.

Through his life, because he was human, Jesus provides Christians with the perfect example of how they should live.

Through his death, because he was God, Jesus could resolve the problem of sin and human failure.

Through his resurrection, he conquers death. He shows God's total power over death.

Faith and works

What Christians believe about salvation affects their daily life. It particularly affects their attitude towards the relationship between their beliefs and their actions, or what the New Testamant calls 'faith' and 'works'. If people believe that their faith in Jesus is what saves them, they might see no need to lead a good life. If they believe that their actions are what saves them, they may think that beliefs do not matter. Most Christians believe it is important to combine the two – leading a good life as well as believing in Jesus.

I

Heaven is God's gift to anyone who believes in Jesus, repents of sin and asks God's forgiveness.

God is a welcoming God. All people, from all religions, will go to heaven.

You can earn your place in heaven by living a good life.

God has already decided who will go to heaven.

1 Which of the views in Source I is closest to your own? Why?

2 James Hogg, a 19th-century novelist, wrote *The Private Memoirs and Confessions of a Self-justified Sinner*, in which he explored what might happen if a person believed that faith mattered for everything, and actions did not matter at all. Create a short story or sketch based around this or the opposite belief. Your teacher can tell you what happened in James Hogg's story. You can compare your ideas with his.

✓ CHECKPOINT
A Second Coming?
Many Christians believe that Jesus will return to Earth at the time of Judgement – the Second Coming. This belief is affirmed by Christians each time they say the *Apostles' Creed*. The basis for this belief is found in Acts 1.6–11 where Jesus' ascension to heaven is described. Jesus will be involved in Judgement, but when and where this may take place is not known.

Ready to die?

You might expect their belief in life after death to make Christians feel positive about dying! Sources J and K give two different perspectives on this.

J

Tie the strings to my life,
    my Lord,
Then I am ready to go!
Just a look at the horses –
Rapid! That will do!

Put me on the firmest side,
So I shall never fall;
For we must ride to the
Judgement,
    and it's partly downhill.

But never I mind the
    bridges
And never I mind the sea;
Held fast in everlasting
    race
By my own choice and thee.

Good-bye to the life
    I used to live,
And the world I used to
    know;
And kiss the hills for me,
    just once;
Now I am ready to go!

Emily Dickinson (1830–86)

K

Q: Say one of your congregation has been bereaved – what do you try to do?
A: People go through stages after someone they love has died. They feel shock and anger. Then they may deny those strong feelings. Another stage is regret. They think, 'If only I'd done this or that before they died …' These are all natural stages. You can't hurry people through them. They are part of accepting the situation.

Q: But surely it's different for Christians who believe in life after death than for people who don't.
A: Not really. At least, the experience of grief is actually surprisingly similar. The stages are the same for those who believe in life after death as for those who don't. Because grief is a human emotion. You can feel angry at someone leaving you even if you feel you are going to see them again in heaven when you eventually die.

Q: You do a lot of funerals. Is there such a thing as a happy funeral?
A: Yes there is. I can remember one funeral I did for a family – the husband had died suddenly of a heart attack after only 18 months of marriage. The funeral was in the churchyard not in the church because the man – Pete – did not like churches but he did like the open air. The step-son, who had been very close to Pete and was feeling really angry about Pete dying, insisted on helping carry the coffin. He was a thin 16-year-old, and he struggled with the heavy coffin. The undertakers said he shouldn't be allowed to do it, but he wanted to and I allowed it. He sweated and swore his way through it and it was worth it. It was important to him to go through with this.
Around the graveside people shared their memories of Pete. One man who had been his best man 18 months earlier held an imaginary conversation with Pete – full of jokes, but full of feeling too.

Q: But why was this happy?
A: Well it was celebrating someone's life. But it was honest. No one was trying to hide their real feelings. They were using the funeral as a way of working through those feelings.

Q: Are the British particularly uptight about death?
A: Yes! It shows in our funerals and the way we mourn. In other cultures, in the Orthodox tradition, for example, they display the dead body. They touch it, even kiss it. They cry, uncontrollably if that's how they feel. I've had people say to me in Britain: 'My biggest fear is that I will cry at the funeral!' That's awful. Expressing emotion should be part and parcel of the funeral.

Q: What 'Christian messages' do you give at funerals?
A: I have two favourite themes. One of the best is the scene in the Bible when Mary Magdalene meets Jesus after he has risen from the dead. She wants to hold on to him and hug him. He lets her, but then he says something like, 'Don't cling to me!' That's a wonderful picture of what we must do: let go of the person who died.
The Bible is full of comfort for the bereaved. In Revelation there is a picture of a world with no more crying or mourning or sadness. It's a powerful symbol of the hope people have for the future.
But the real thing about funerals is that people do not remember what you say, or what the service says. They remember the feeling with which you led the funeral – your hope, or your hardness – the pictures you leave in their minds.

An interview with Dilly Baker, a priest in an ecumenical church in Milton Keynes. She has specialised in counselling the bereaved.

Life before death

'We believe in life before death' is Christian Aid's mission statement – summarising their work (see page 70). This expresses another Christian hope for the future: that, when faced by evil and suffering in this world, the most Christian response is not to promise people a perfect afterlife, but to work to improve their lives now – to bring a heaven on Earth.

Jesus often talks about the Kingdom of Heaven. In Matthew's Gospel he begins many parables by saying, 'The Kingdom of Heaven is like this ...' However, he does not describe what heaven looks like or where it might be found. Instead, he explains what kind of behaviour characterises the Kingdom of Heaven and who will get in.

Many Christians believe that Jesus' teaching about the Kingdom of Heaven is more important as a guide to their behaviour in this life than in a possible future. The passages show Christians how they might try to bring the Kingdom of Heaven into this world.

L

FOCUS TASK

The Sermon on the Mount
The collection of teachings in Matthew 5–7 contains some of the most inspirational words in the New Testament. You are going to prepare a Sermon on the Mount display for your classroom. This will help you to understand the teaching it contains, as well as providing a useful resource for your revision.

1 **As a class, read through the whole sermon (Matthew 5–7).**
2 **Divide it into sections, using the headings in the Bible to help you.**
3 **Divide into groups – each group taking one section of the sermon.**
   a) **On a large sheet of paper write the heading: 'The Kingdom of Heaven is like this ...'**
   b) **Work out how to summarise your section in language that could be understood by a 10-year-old child. Write your summary in large letters on the sheet.**
   c) **Add appropriate illustrations if you wish.**
4 **As a class, arrange all the sheets in an agreed order.**
5 **Re-read your new version of the Sermon on the Mount, checking that everyone understands it and that no important points have been missed.**

*Then I saw a new heaven
and a new earth.
The first heaven
and the first earth
had gone.
No longer
'pie in the sky'
for the oppressed of the earth.
Heaven and earth
had come together
here
and
now.
They were no longer
separated.
I saw the city,
Egoli:
place of gold,
polished and
shining brightly.
And I heard a voice say:
'We are free at last'.
God has answered us,
making a home with us.
No more Group Areas:
black and white
live together.
And God
lives among us,
wiping away our tears.
No more deaths;
women will not weep over the dead,
children will not cry as orphans,
men will not abuse power:
those things are done with.
For all things are being made new.*

*The constitution
is being re-written
by the people.
The one who is
the beginning
and end
has made our stories
one.
We were thirsty for justice,
but even in deep trouble
hope sprung up in us.
Now it has bubbled over.
We have received
what our ancestors
lived
and
died
for.
We are all children of the Living One
forever.*

Written by Janet Lees after the 1994 South African general election in which 50 years of overtly racist, white-minority government was brought to an end

Arguments about God – Review tasks

A

1 Give an account in your own words of the Bible's Creation story from Genesis 1 and 2.
2 Describe two contrasting Christian attitudes towards this Creation story.
3 Explain with reference to Genesis 1–3 what is happening in the picture.
4 How might the story of Adam and Eve help a Christian explain the following:
  a) suffering in this world
  b) the existence of evil?
4 How might a Christian explain the significance of Jesus in resolving the problems of suffering and evil?

B

1 Does the picture show an example of sacramental worship or charismatic worship?
2 Explain how either sacramental worship or charismatic worship might help a Christian to know God.
3 How else might Christians of different traditions find out God's will for them?
4 'Religious experience is the best way of knowing God.' Explain how far Christians would agree with this statement, showing that you have considered other points of view.

C

1 Describe three features of a Christian belief in life after death.
2 Explain two ways in which Christians might disagree in their views on this subject.
3 How might a Christian's belief in life after death affect their behaviour in this life?
4 'Jesus died for the sins of the whole world.'
  a) How might Christians respond to this statement?
  b) What is your personal view of this statement? Explain your answer.

Conclusion

You've reached the end of your course. How will it be useful to you?

Your exam

Your chief concern is probably to get a good grade in your exam. We have helped you in various ways. Here is a reminder of the ideas you will need to bear in mind when you revise for your exam.

Different traditions

Christians have a range of views. There is no one single, unified Christian opinion. In your exam, you will need to show that you understand this and that you are aware of the way Christian traditions take different attitudes to moral and theological issues.

You will improve your grade if you can show your grasp of the differences between Christian traditions, or between Christianity and another religion, on moral issues.

Sources of authority

You have examined the ways Christians use sources such as the Bible or their church leaders as authorities.

You will improve your grade if you can show not only the sources of authority used by different Christians, but also how they use each source of authority.

Absolute and relative

You have investigated the difference between an absolutist approach to morality and a relativist approach and have recorded your own examples of absolutist and relativist responses to different issues.

You will improve your grade if you can refer to absolutist and relativist morality confidently. You should show you understand that they are not watertight definitions; rather, they show an 'approach' to decision making on certain issues by certain traditions.

Core beliefs

You have studied some of the core beliefs that lie at the heart of Christian thinking on moral issues, such as stewardship and the sanctity of life.

You will improve your grade if you can not only describe such beliefs, but also demonstrate how these beliefs inspire Christians and affect their values and their actions. Christianity is a living faith, evolving and changing year by year as its followers meet new challenges. The course is about real-life Christianity. It is your understanding of the relationship between these beliefs and Christian values and actions that will interest the examiner.

Your own views

This course has given you plenty of opportunity to express your own views and to give reasons for them. You may be surprised that even this will be useful in your exam.

Sometimes you are specifically asked for your view in an exam question. The **reasons** for your opinion, and your ability to back it up, interest the examiner more than the viewpoint itself. So, remember: you will improve your grade if you can express your own views on issues you have tackled, and explain and support them with reference to the Christian ideas you have studied in this book.

Your beliefs and values

One of the aims of Religious Education is to learn from religion. Religion gives its followers beliefs and values to live by. This course has encouraged you to debate, to understand and to make your own decisions about Christian beliefs and values. The beliefs and values you have studied in this course may be similar to your own or they may be different. In either case, this course should have helped you to clarify your own beliefs and values.

FOCUS TASK

The illustration shows some values that Christians might think were important to help guide people in their moral decision making.
1   Choose three that you would like to take with you into the future. Explain your choice.
2   Explain whether you reject any of the values altogether and, if so, why.
3   For your three chosen values, draw a diagram similar to the one on page 8, giving an example of how they might affect your actions in the future.

RE-EVALUATION

4   At the beginning of this book you recorded your own views on the relevance of religion to life in the modern world. Has your view changed at all? If so, how and why?

Subject index

A

abortion 15–19
Abortion Act (1968) 15, 17
adoption 18, 19
adultery 35, 36, 37
afterlife 121–5, 126
agnostic 90, 91, 93
AIDS 47
Anglican Church 6, 7, 55; *see also* Church of England
animal rights 80
anthropomorphism 101
apartheid 50
Apostles' Creed 106
Aquinas, St Thomas 84, 92, 93
arms trade 86
atheist 90, 91, 93
Augustine, St 57, 119
authority 5, 10, 61

B

Baptist Church 6
beliefs 8–9, 90–91
Bible
    interpretation of 7
    New International Version 57
Big Bang Theory 92, 93, 96

C

Campaign Against Arms Trade 86
capital punishment 26–31
    Death Row 31
Catholic Church 6, 18, 22, 26, 37, 39, 42, 43, 55, 56, 80, 111, 112, 113
Catholics 5, 22, 109
celibacy 39
Charismatic Movement 112
charismatic worship 112
Christian Aid 70–71, 126
Christianity
    spread of 6–7
    world view 8–10
Churches' Commission for Racial Justice 49
Church of England 6, 7, 53, 54–5, 61, 62, 84
Church of Scotland 43, 69
civil war 84, 85
cohabitation 35, 45

Committee for Minority Ethnic Anglican Concerns 53
conscience 5, 72
conscientious objectors 85
contraception 15, 18, 37, 42
conversion 112
compassion 17, 18, 20, 24, 48, 72
covenant (*see also* marriage) 43
Creationism 97
Creation story 50, 76, 92, 96, 97
Crusades 83

D

Darwin, Charles 95, 97
death 125; *see also* euthanasia
Death Row 31
design, argument of 94–5
discrimination 49–53, 54–9
divorce 35, 43–4
Dunblane massacre 114–15, 118
Dutch Reformed Church of South Africa (DRC) 50
Dutch Reformed Mission Church (DRMC) 50

E

embryos, destruction of 12–14
environmental issues 71, 76–80
Epicurus 95
Eucharist 113
euthanasia 20–25
evangelical Christians 5, 7, 17, 40, 44, 45, 48, 55, 103, 109, 112
Evangelical Churches 98
evil 115, 118–20, 126
evolution, theory of 95
EXIT (Voluntary Euthanasia Society) 20
experience, religious 98–9, 109, 110, 112–13

F

Faith in the City 62
family life 40–42
Faslane Peace Camp Scottish Christians 85
free will 20, 22, 114, 117, 118, 119

G

General Synod of the Church of England 53, 54, 78
George Macleod Centre, Iona 69
God
    existence, proofs of
        Design argument 94–5
        First Cause argument 92–3
        religious experiences 98–9, 112
    nature of 100–107
    revelation of 108–13
Golden Rule 10

H

heaven 121, 122, 126
hell 123
Hindley, Myra 30
Hippocratic oath 21, 24
Holocaust 119
Holy Spirit 112
holy war 83
homosexuality 45–8
hospices 24
House Church movement 112
Humanae Vitae ('On Human Life') 17
hunting 80

I

immanence 102, 104, 106, 110
impersonal (God) 102–3, 104, 106
Iona Community 69
Islam 105
IVF (in vitro fertilisation) 12

J

Jesus 104
    death of 117, 124
    incarnation of 106
    nature of 106
    resurrection of 106, 124
Job, suffering of 116
Judaism 6, 105
justice 27, 57, 62–3, 72, 84
just war 84, 85

People index